TWEEN PLACE

TWEEN PLACE

The journey through

TIFFANY MAYS

Tween Place

Copyright © 2021 by Tiffany Mays. All rights reserved.

No part of this publication may be reproduced, stored in a retrieval system or transmitted in any way by any means, electronic, mechanical, photocopy, recording or otherwise without the prior permission of the author except as provided by USA copyright law.

The opinions expressed by the author are not necessarily those of URLink Print and Media.

1603 Capitol Ave., Suite 310 Cheyenne, Wyoming USA 82001
1-888-980-6523 | admin@urlinkpublishing.com

URLink Print and Media is committed to excellence in the publishing industry.

Book design copyright © 2021 by URLink Print and Media. All rights reserved.

Published in the United States of America

Library of Congress Control Number: 2020926018

ISBN 978-1-64753-619-0 (Paperback)
ISBN 978-1-64753-620-6 (Digital)

04.05.21

Dedication

I would like to dedicate this book to my mother, Earnestine Mays. I will carry you in my heart and spirit always. Thank you for being the wonderful mother you are and introducing me to Christ Jesus. I love you.

Table of Contents

Introduction 9
Reality Check 13
The Resistance 21
The Pathways 35
Detours 45
Self-Justifications 51
The Void 59
The Dance 71
The Battle 77
The Rebirth 93
The Outlet 99
Training Day 105
Taking Back Destiny 119
Embracing Destiny.. 127

INTRODUCTION

Life brings many unpredictable moments that leave unseen effects on the way we live. Questions of why things are happening surface to our lips asking, when did my life begin to go wrong? When did it all start, and when will it end? Why has my life stop moving forward? What is this place, and how can I get out? We are all victims of causalities, and by identifying the causes, we could get to the effect.

How many of us can honestly say we even remember the things that shaped our present life, although we are living the results. Who would have ever thought that a tiny lesson of cause and effect in those school age years could render lifelong lessons? Many of life's lessons leave unanswered questions. Creating a foundation filled with personalities taken on through suppressed emotions and failures due to lack of knowledge. Life takes us down multiple paths that seem to leave the mistaken impression that we are moving forward, when in all actuality we are traveling in circles.

Pathways disguised to look like different faces and places. All the while, we are dancing and getting older with each new song. When asking questions to become aware of your surroundings, you find no one to help you. Hell seems to be breaking loose in your life, making you feel like everyone is watching you burn. Next you began a cycle of panic and frustration, being in this state of mind forces a reaction that cannot be ignored. I experienced denial, trying to pretend those situations were not happening to me.

Denial made me feel more pain, confusion, and loneliness. I started to fight in every situation that allowed me to vent, even if it had nothing to do with what I was going through. I searched out weakness in others so no one could see my weaknesses. I never once looked to a higher power to help me find my way or trusted even the closest family members with my secrets. Desperate situations made for desperate actions which led to desperate shouts for help, to all the wrong people.

When the responds of those you are asking for help is not what you expected, the cycle begins all over again. It takes a huge amount of strength to ask for help only to get a responds like "you're crazy" or simply "stressed out". You begin to believe, the advice of others and seek to do it, this advice never shows the way off this particular path. False dependences begin to form giving people a sense of power over you, rendering no results. Yet again another trap you have to escape from, when in this Place. In this place many people share pieces of you; causing you to take on false obligations to be there for others when you are not even there for yourself.

When attempting to give yourself over to love you fail, not realizing how out of control life has become. When in this Place self-awareness is absent, and the approval addiction is present. Leaving us puzzled to think, are we building up on a foundation of painful experiences? Will it ultimately lead to indecisiveness? Why can't I move forward? Why can't I seem to make good choices? We must expose this Place, which harbors our heartache and confusion by facing up to it. Every one of us has a destine assignment to fulfill in the Earth, a grand design put into place.

Walking out that set path, headed into the right direction, unlocks the release of peace for your soul. When we are blinded to our pain, we are also blinded to the solution. In this book we can shine light on your pain and seek out the absolution you have been waiting for. In the beginning, God had a plan for the Earth; unfortunately disobedience caused that plan to change. (Genesis 3:1-6) Sin was ushered into the

Earth and a place that was once pure, holy, and righteous became the opposite. The Earth became a double standard, split into two different life forces causing it to become the Tween Place. I believe this broke the heart of God, along with the consequences of their mistake.

The Earth once had a purpose, it lacked no good thing. Adam and Eve caused themselves and the world to become separated from its Creator. This great separation caused a huge ripple in the ocean of human life. (Genesis 3:7) He gave them His grace, and mercy. He could have killed them both but He loved them just as He loves you and me. When God questioned Adam about the incident, Adam quickly blamed his wife then God for giving her to him. (Genesis 3:12)

How quick are we in blaming others for our choices? There was another involved in the beginnings of our shame and the causing of this Tween Place to arise, the serpent. He was punished for his assistance in the act of betrayal. (Genesis 3:14) God cursed the serpent to crawl on his belly as if he was eating dust. With that curse, the serpent slithered away. I believe, in that moment, the Earth transformed from Heaven on Earth to a Tween Place, a place between good and evil, where purity of neither exists. Evil cannot conquer it can only influence, and good cannot fully exist but can sustain us. Neither one can fully take over while in this Tween Place. After these incidents took place, God desired to fix the broken union.

The Earth in this form was not God's plan. It was not meant to exist in a double standard, providing only temporary life. It was not created to house division, war, and sickness. It was not created to witness death. It was created for wholeness. It was created for eternal fellowship with the Creator. Eternal life ended when the sin of disobedience entered the Earth that day in the garden. Sin did not extend the life of man, but it killed our rights to life (Roman 6:21) Knowing your beginning creates a foundation to build upon, truth is necessary.

Truth is the key to survival in the Earth, you must learn the "what's, and why's" of life. It affects everything you are and everything you do. Realizing something is missing and wrong with the puzzle of life cannot continually be ignored. We cannot wait for someone to fill in the pieces for us; we must begin to seek out the answers for ourselves. Begin asking questions, anything to get beyond ourselves so we can receive the truth and illumination of God's mercy. God had a plan to save us all those many years ago, come with me as I reveal the Master's plan. Only He can save us from the final judgment of the Tween Place.

REALITY CHECK

Reality can never be an easy thing to face especially when we believe it is being lived. Every day you awake in a life you feel is good, bad or not so great thinking this is your reality, but that is not so. Our reality travels a lot deeper than what we see or think we are living. Society has learned to take the easier route in life and to forget about the things we are lacking and go after only what we know exist. We make conscience efforts to do as we are taught then on occasion what we want.

Throughout life, we learn many powerful lessons, not all of them come from school, but everyday life. How can one truly know if they have indeed learned a lesson? I believe each day teaches us something new about ourselves? Some days bright light shines on the dark places in our life. How many can say they are living the realities of their life? Are we suppressing life true story because it's too painful to bear? When I think on life and all the many ways of life that I have been exposed to, I wonder who is living out their life in reality. I work hard daily to stay in reality and not allow my mind to slip away into day dreams and unrealistic expectations.

What makes up reality? Where can it be found? How is one to know when their reality is found? Life with its many ingredients becomes so very confusing to put together you have no idea how it will turn out once it's done. Once reality is discovered is it the reality we could united in? Wow, wouldn't it be great if there was such a reality.

What if I told you such a reality exist? A reality not created by the circumstances of your life, but one that is created by your inherited right. I have come into the knowledge of an astonishing reality check, and I would like to share it with you. I do not pretend to know all the answers. I only give to you what I am meant to give, nothing more. I would like to open up your soul to more than just your life, but to the choices and consequences that shaped our presence life. Anything in the beginning that was put into place for our good, man with his deceitful heart and educated mind has corrupted.

Even the best things in life that we as a people feel is protected, those are the very things that are at risk of corruption. We tend to be a very over confident people always thinking we have it all under control. The most powerful among us still has to answer to someone for his/her decisions. The reality check of life comes in like that of a storm; we all have a higher power to give an account of deeds done and deeds undone. What would it be like to reach the end of life and still be unfulfilled, how tragic that must be! What is it to be fulfilled? We run from the very things in life that would fulfill us simply because they are unfamiliar, but not really unfamiliar, just not sought after.

When familiar, destiny becomes just like breathing, and the great design of your life comes naturally. Destiny needs to be sought out, before we were formed in the womb it was imparted in us (Jeremiah 1:5), the essence of our spirit, destiny makes up who we really are. Destiny is just another word for message. Who are we really? We are messengers sent out on a very important assignment to deliver what was given to us at the beginning of all things. This is why the bible speaks of the body being a temple and to keep it holy. You have precious cargo, and it must be handled with care.

The reality check is that you do not belong to yourself but you belong to who sent you. Your beginning and end has been seen by only one, and that is God, there is none like Him, His purpose will stand. (Isaiah 46:9, 10) Education of those schools like things and learning your one, two, and three's are needed but do not help in the guiding to destiny. Destiny is the message inside of me, and I'm the carrier, so what is the search for? Just as a treasure box need a key so do we? So in all reality the question is; where is the key? How do I get unlock? The key is not far or even hidden from us, we do not need a treasure map to find it. All we need is to make a decision to receive the truth of our existence, and face life in all its realities.

In order to do this we must walk, live and breathe in the reality of our circumstances. What is truly going on and why, part of doing that is acceptance of our history. Meaning the beginning of days when Adam and Eve walked the Earth and was in constant communion with God. Accepting what went wrong and embracing God's new plan for our lives. Exposing the Tween Place by accepting its history, and do away with the building of small kingdoms, we can begin. This place holds all the hurts and disappointments you have experienced, it is holding you prisoner, it is not your home, it is simply a temporary dwelling place.

The reality is, everyday lived in this Tween Place you are a captive and there is only one way out. It's like being plugged into a system design to ultimately destroy you. Accepting your beginnings is vital to your freedom for without acceptance of your beginnings you are denying yourself the right to fight in a battle that will determine your very fate. The reality of God's plan for us is eternal life with Him. He wants to fellowship with us every minute of every day for all eternity, but we have to make a choice. A choice to seek out the reality of life, to get past ourselves to get to destiny. God has a grand design in order that every single human being will know His Son therefore know Him.

The Tween Place only has power when we refuse to face up to the reality of how we are living. God tells us in His Word to "seek and we shall find" "knock and the door will open", all we need is to search out the truth, when in doubt read the Word of God, all you need is there. To sit around in a zombie like state of mind in absolute wonder and deep thought is not seeking, nor is debating, picking up the Word of God is action. Here's another reality check, we walk through life in complete denial that part of us is indeed supernatural. Our spiritual being that goes through life totally neglected and only thought of when we die.

The only persons with definite proof to the truth that the spirit being actually exist is the persons who dies, and are unable to communicate such a discovery. Still, it is hard to wrap your mind around that statement, never fear the Word of God comes to bring clarity to the most trivial doubts. (Ephesians 4:1-5) That is why I feel God has given us insight to the mysteries of our very being and why we exist. To accept the reality of who you really are will get you to a place in life were God can reveal his mysteries. A decision has to be made, to get out of our own way and learn His way to see what we have been blinded to all our lives. I have a mystery to reveal to help aid on this new found reality, we have been over the "Earth" and what happened with it, now there is another, unlike the Earth that's not in plain view.

Acceptance of your beginnings will help in digesting these powerful truths. There is also a dimension of the spirit. When the Earth was converted to a Tween place because of sin the battle of good and evil kicked off like that of a football game, and we the human race have been dead in the center, whether we want to admit it or not, if you have been on this Earth and dwell here on Earth you are on a battlefield. Somewhere along the line the message of what is really going on got a bit mixed up. That is why this book is being written to bring in some clarity.

We here in America know all too well the damage of war. Can you imagine what a war looks like when only the other country is fighting and we are standing looking lost and confused? I know, even I cannot imagine the defeat or casualties. Oh, I could just hear the despair and anguish of those who were to be protected, but let down because no one acknowledged they were in a war. All is the same in this reality check I am sharing right now, to ignore that you indeed are part supernatural is to deny your very defense against a very real enemy. To open your mind up to the realm of the spirit is to not only help you in the discovery of your true self, but the discovery of a very powerful enemy. Our enemy is only powered through our refusal to acknowledge his existence. Reality check, you can continue to live life walking in the darkness of mistakes to accept only what life throws at you, or turn on the light. Yes, I know light shows off everything kept secret, hidden, and those things that are consider to be ugly, but I would prefer to expose all my hidden identities than to be beat over the head with life's downfalls and could do nothing simply because I cannot see it coming. That is exactly what happens when you deny yourself what is rightfully yours. Here's another reality check for you, when the Earth was converted those long years ago we lost a lot and things got changed up a bit. What we lost was that direct know how, the relationship with God, were Adam had Him at his side. Adam had no need to fight or anything, God definitely had his back.

One thing I feel was in that time of Adam that we still have is the right to choose. When the serpent came to Eve and deceived her, all he had was his smooth words. Those words had no power until after she bit the apple and convince Adam to do so as well. What power did he gain you ask? He gain the power of influence in the Tween Place, he had no power in the Earth before the sin occurred. Adam and Eve gave him that foot hold in the Tween Place. This serpent is not someone or something that the Bible never mentions; it speaks about this deceitful creature in a different text and explains his little trick of influence (Revelation 12:3). Not only was he a serpent, he has been labeled a dragon and an angel before becoming all these monstrous creatures of deceit. He was once known as a worshipping angel whom thought himself greater than God his creator. His power of influence was active and most destructive in the time of Adam and Eve. How much more destructive has he become now in the present?

He influenced one-third of Heaven to challenge God for the throne, to actually join in with him to fight God and take over the Heavens. Can you imagine what type of battle that was? (Revelation 12:7-12) You do not have to imagine, I will tell you, it was not much of one he was defeated very quickly and all those along with him. They were cast down to the Earth, you see we are not alone, nor are we completely human we are indeed part supernatural. Whether we choose to accept who we are or not the battle will still go on. The dragon a.k.a. Satan is angry and on a mission to destroy the entire human race, he does not see color or gender he sees your soul and he wants it badly.

You not acknowledging you even having a soul will not save you from his wrath it will simply make it easier for him. Reality check, time is not on our side; in fact the days are going so quickly who can keep up. We must get serious about the truth of our existence and seek to find what God wants to give. We have to make a decision to stop fighting the truth. It is time to seek it out, simply not believing me is not a good enough reason to stop looking, the answers are out there, if you could not find them here, I encourage you to keep looking you must not give up your soul depends upon it.

Now let's talk about the change in plan that God had to make due to those unfortunate events in the beginning. Due to men sinful heart God had to find a way to bring our wayward mind and deceitful heart back into repentance and fellowship with Him. (John 3:16) This passage of scripture tells us the plan for the redemption of man. God did something so extraordinary, He sent us His only Son Jesus Christ. You see in the beginnings the horrible temptation of the serpent caused all of mankind to be damn to death, to live a life dictated by the circumstances of sin, bound by its fate of death. When God sent His son Jesus the Savior He came that we can have life, more than just life, but eternal life. Understanding what God did leads to the truth of the supernatural being inside you and me.

Living in this Earth without the purpose of the Creator, you are not living at all, just existing. Merely existing is not such a good fate when everything around you is being dictated by an unseen force of evil. Just because we refuse to fight does not mean we will be ignored by the enemy. Understanding the realms of good and evil is most important and cannot be taken lightly; it must be walked out boldly. Reality check, how many of us wait until something dreadful happens to us before we seek out the protection of an unseen force of good, oh yes, that is when we pray and convince ourselves that we believe in the unseen. Faith floats to the surface, destroying the seed of unbelief, and opening the door of understanding to all His Word. You may ask. What is it that I need to be set free from? Sin, the illusion of life in the Earth, and all the offspring that have been born through the millions of sins committed.

We as a people are in great need of deliverance; we are in trouble and in great need of an awakening. You may ask. What exactly do we need to wake up from? A lifetime of sleeping and dreaming of what we want, and building kingdoms on soil that has been cursed. Earth has a purpose to be the battleground, not for us to make a wealthy life here; we do not even know what to do with the wealth in our hands, but to buy more things to enhance our mini kingdoms. In seeking out the truth about who we really are we can find ourselves right where He paid the price to give us back eternal life at the cross. Jesus gave his life on the cross that we may live and not die.

God sent his Son for this ultimate sacrifice to save us, His Son is from Heaven were He dwells which makes Him supernatural. Why would God send His Son to die for a people who are not supernatural, He was sent because we are indeed supernatural and through His death had been made whole again. Jesus ushered the portion of good in the Earth that was lacking due to the sin and sickness that had spread throughout the world. That is what His Earthly death did for us, in the realm of Spirit he took back the key of life and death from Satan, He granted eternal life as a gift to anyone who believes in Him, and by believing you trust Him. By trusting you have allowed Him to show you the way through the Tween Place, and to destroy the tricks and plots of the enemy.

The enemy and his many disguises and let us not forget the power of influence. He has a lot of tricks up his sleeve that get more and more creative with each new moon. Ignoring our power and assignment causes us to wonder around in the dark going to our nine's to five's everyday like little robots. Satan is hoping to keep us in this zombie like state of mind, to keep us focused on trying to gain the riches of the world that he witnessed curse and knows all too well its fate. Reality check, what is it for a man to gain the entire world and lose his soul? We need to wake up, look into the mirror right now and say "reality check"! The tactics of the enemy are useless against a vessel that sees him for who he is.

The weapons of power are in understanding what you are fighting against. Who can defeat something they know nothing about or cannot even see? To believe in Christ Jesus and allow Him to reveal who you are, is also allowing Him to reveal the enemy. You cannot have one without the other, wanting to know the enemy without embracing Christ is like welcoming death. Reality check, in understanding your why's, what's, how's, and when's starts your journey. By accepting Christ in your heart and believing God sent His only Son to give your life back is your first step toward the ultimate reality, and to whom much is given, much is required.

Let us begin to face it, God has given us much, and there is work to do, much work to do, remember you are on a battlefield. Allow your mind and your spirit to receive what is being revealed in this book. As God did for me, let Him open your eyes and set your spirit free so you can truly reap the rewards this life has to offer, but a choice has to be made. Have you made yours, or are you in a resistance?

The Resistance

We dealt briefly with denial in chapter 1, but as we go further I will be explaining more in detail the very depths of how harmful and life threatening this particular phase can be. Denial is like a poison to the soul, seeking to destroy but only able to injure. Denial causes a total and complete hindrance to God's plan for your life. Resistance and denial are so close in relation they could be mother and daughter. Denial has many disguises but is most powerful when in its true form.

When refusing to see truth even when its directly in view can be an example of someone being set in their own way of thinking and dealing. This could demonstrate denial in it's truest form. When in denial one's perception of whats happening to them is alter, by a false reality in which they are able to cope. Many of life lessons prepare us for the exact questions we ask and struggle over. This could answer more than one concern that you may encounter while reading my book, why do women have to go through so much and when will it end? God has an answer for everything we go through and has revealed those answers in His Word. The state of resistance is the reason for the disconnect. It happens when seeking an exact answer through His Word. We are unable to draw from a true place to discover the heart of what we are feeling and going through because of our alternate state of mind like an alternate world created to resist the true reality causing a false impression and feelings etc... hindering your right to a real question. Therefore when you seek answers in the Word of God you cannot find what you need, you don't really know what you actually need. In denial no questions are real, its like looking for buried treasure with a fake map.

Denial is a continual cycle that is always revolving, and could be never ending. Denial leads straight into that brick wall of resistance. Denial in its true form always delivers off-springs and resistance happens to be one of them. There is an escape to this cycle of death, but first let's discover its fruits. People that I have crossed paths with will know me for saying what I am about to share with you. That there are some lessons in life that your mom or dad could warn you about and you would actually listen and then there are other lessons that God Himself could warn us against and yet we do them anyway. Some lessons have to be lived not told. Meaning no matter how many people tell you not to do something you have to live out the experience to know what was right or wrong.

Living out these lessons in life leaves us with such a complex that we forget about the consequences behind choosing to go against the voice of wisdom when advice was given. You may not come out on the other side as you entered, most come out mature, focus, and cautious. Some not so lucky, they come out torn, broken, paranoid, and stricken with grief, sorrow, and never quite able to put the pieces back together again. In this condition it is hard to gather thoughts on what exactly happened and to see the lesson in it all. There are so many mixed emotions that we as women go through, we don't know whether to be angry or to scream out in wails of sorrow, to close ourselves off, or to hide behind bad habits, like cigarettes, alcohol, drugs, or sex. Although these are definitely the results of a state of denial it is not the end.

Life here on this planet does not have to be filled with hate, resentment, addictions, and depression. There is a peace that surpasses all understanding. I can show you the way. How can we identify this deadly snake that slithers up to us to devour our soul for damnation? Remember the many disguises of the enemy, denial will be one of his tricks, and that skill is at work right now throughout the nation.

Resistance has this amazing crippling effect on the mind, blocking new found knowledge and wisdom with its influences. It looks for past memories, mistakes, and hurts to fill its plan against you. Resistance could be described as an entity with an assignment to destroy you. Keeping you in a place where truth cannot be received while you are continually aging rapidly and eventually perishing. In your final moments of life, the truth of everything the resistance has blocked you from will come back like a spirit of truth in a form of a memory to haunt your refusal to see the truth. The power in defeating such a clever entity is to know it traits and check yourself for clues, or have someone you trust give you a snapshot of your character, but be careful it take wisdom and discernment to know whom is truly trustable.

We discovered in chapter 1 the dimensions of good and evil; now let us focus on how they work. Resistance is not a force of good but a tool of the enemy to keep you tied up so he can live his plan throughout your life using your body. The bodies that we as human being were born into are called our "flesh" the part of us that make up the DNA. Both the flesh and the spirit were affected by Adam's and Eve's decision to go against God in the Garden of Eden. Things got split into half and we got put in between. This action of Adam and Eve caused everything to become a double standard, even us. Now I can imagine God thinking how to get us back to him after this act of betrayal happened.

I believe that the part of us that is good is called the spirit and it is untouched by the corruption of this Tween Place. Our spirit is the part of us that came purely from the lungs of God Himself. In the beginning God created Adam and blew into him the spirit of life. Just as he did for Adam he did for us, and as Adam became separated from God when he choose to eat from the forbidden tree so did we, the future of mankind was affected, also cursed with the consequences of our ancestors, but only in body not in spirit. You see Adam and Eve caused a fleshly separation from God not a spiritual one, which is unbreakable. Nevertheless it was a tremendous loss. We once had both the physical and spiritual connection all in one, we were eternal.

God has been and always attempts to gather back the eternal connection ever since it was lost. He fore knew the danger we inherited from the disobedient act causing mankind to become preyed upon by evil that dwell on the Earth. It hurt Him so badly to watch the enemy attempting to destroy all that He loves. He had to put an outlet in the Earth to get us out of danger. In the beginnings God hovered over the children of Israel to guide them. He gave to them a leader by the name of Moses, whom He communicated through to guide the children of Israel to the Promised Land.

In His efforts to redeem the lost connection the people of Israel choose to resist the voice of guidance and their attempts to reach the Promised Land alone without God failed. As will our attempts to survive in this Tween Place without the guidance of God we will perish. The power of influence the enemy had in the Earth was taking a hold of so many God was losing us one by one. Sin was taking over and destroying everything regardless of what God was saying through his prophets and leaders Israel had become a rebellion nation of people who ignore God's voice. They became deluded with their own selfish reasons for living and because they could not see God face to face they even questioned if he was indeed real. Surrendering themselves over to a delusion of what a God is they begin to build false gods to worship.

Ignoring the one true God who delivered them out of the hands of Pharaoh by whom many had already died, still they did not believe. Israel had become a resistance nation of people and with their resistance of the truth came about a great consequence; a generation left to wonder in the wilderness for the rest of their fleshly life until the end, and I am sure that the spirit of truth visited each one and revealed all that was denied. You see denial has huge consequences, resistance to the truth is not all your fault it has a reason for being in your mind. Let's see, Ask yourself who am I?

The answer is you are both made up of spirit and of flesh, but which of these two are in control. You are made up of DNA, that of your ancestors and parents. So if you really think about it, you are a lot of people, so how do you find yourself in all your family tree. The real you is on the inside it is the very part that cannot be contaminated by this world or your DNA it is the spirit. The spirit is your true self it is exactly who God intended for you to be, not your family tree of bad habits, and sickness. You have a pure quality an identity lying silently inside of you waiting for you to acknowledge its presence.

Resistance takes you away from this reality and keeps you fixed on what you see so connecting with yourself can truly be hidden from you. Do you ever wonder why sometimes you act like someone else even if those are qualities in that person you do not like? Being in this form of resistance everything you said, you will not do, or will not say, eventually you will do it. Because in this state you cannot say what you will not do, everything and anything is possible, it's only a matter of time. Remember that slithering snake of influence is waiting patiently to devour his prey and that my love is you.

You have to push pass the denial to reach the place of clarity, begin the search for your reality and watch how fast the denial floods in like that of a storm. To seek out the truth takes strength and we in our flesh like state do not possess it, but guess what happens when you get curious, something inside begins to awaken, that's right, remember that quiet presence inside that is waiting for you to acknowledge it…. yes it awakes. And it begin to help guide you to all the right places and yes I believe it guided you right to this book, if not why do you read it. Some might say that the universe is trying to tell you something, but I believe what is calling us goes beyond the universe, it is our Creator, our Father, the beginning and the end, I believe it is God calling back the part of Him that He blew into us, part of His spirit.

It will be quite a journey to make it back to Him but before we can ever return to Him we must fulfill our purpose in the Earth. There is a great work to be done and knowing your assignment is in the part of you that has to be awakened. Building a resistance to this great power that is waiting to be release in your life can ultimately be the death of your spirit and flesh. When I heard someone say that death is truly the beginning, I understand now what it means, only because the part of me that is needed to return to God has awoken and confirm these words. Life after death is real but life after death has a destination. Good and Evil will be separated in this new place that God is creating for us who has made the choice to come back to Him, evil cannot dwell there.

Like in the beginning of all things, good was everywhere and will be again. The Tween Place will no longer exist; the battle of good and evil will take place. The double standard will no longer exist; the world will not be torn in two, but will be whole again lacking no good thing. You see this entity of denial which yields the offspring of resistance is only another attack to silence the supernatural on the inside and keep you focus on the outside. Life with all it's ups and downs has enough distraction in it to last a lifetime. You may be thinking right now how is it that we are to get pass the distractions and focused long enough to get to the truth of what you speak? It is definitely a process, and the funny thing about this life changing question is how we set ourselves up to fail before we even start to seek out the solution. We wonder through life depressed, struggling with emotional baggage, and the feelings of incompletion, staying their refusing to try. I know how exhausting it must be to search out something that seems so far away or even far fetch to some, but when life treats you like crap because you are living your life according to its rules you must accept the results you are getting.

Living in this Tween Place has its consequences, remember it has a double standard depending on what standard you are living in determines the results you will have to live with. In other words living according to the Earth while on the Earth you are subject to it consequences. To live in the spirit and be guided by the spirit you are no longer subject to results of the Tween Place, you are now on the pathway that yields a great harvest. This harvest is filled with all the nutrients you need to sustain in this Tween Place. The Bible tells us that what we sow we will reap, to sow good seeds in good soil reaps a bountiful harvest, but to sow in bad ground, like living according to this world order, not only are the seeds bad that you are sowing, but the ground as well.

Only God knows where the good and fertile ground is in the Tween Place. The safe places in the Earth are hidden from the evil doers. Those safe places are only exposed to the righteous, God's chosen leaders. Corruption and destruction will inherit this place we spent our existence trying to become something or someone in, absolutely nothing eternal will inhabit this place permanently. Unless we are living in the correct order of our beginnings and accepting its true history we are merely living this life completely in a state of falsehood. We must move forward by facing up to the resistance and accepting the reality of our world the Tween Place.

How many things and false faces have we given in to, so many religious orders, I have already stop counting. The overwhelming need in our society to believe in something has taken the Earth over, and just as those in the beginning took on a different god to worship and not the true God left them unprotected and vulnerable to the tactics of the enemy, we too are to face the same fate if in fact we refuse and continue to resist the truth. Denial of our beginnings gives us over to the wilds of the enemy, having us chasing after false gods, and worshipping things, money, houses, and land in a place where the ground itself is curse.

God desire that we travel light so that the focus of what needs to be done will stay clear, too much stuff creates clutter and your vision becomes alter by what you see, blocking the ability to see clearly what is right in front of you. This is why truth cannot be seen by so many; we have created little kingdoms down here on Earth. Getting side tracked and distracted, thinking we have it all together is a very easy thing to do when so much stuff is blocking our path to truth. We begin holding on to what we think we have, losing full sight of what we are here for.

The resistance that you are experiencing has a lot of stages, it needs fuel to keep you were you are, trust me it is not easy for this little deceiver to keep you in denial it uses everything and everybody to accomplish its goal. An example of a stage would be of your background and how you were brought up, sent to the Earth to be an evangelist for God and end up being a child whose family are unbelievers. This is a battle in itself to bring you into a place where God can expose Himself in a way were you can remember who you are. I call this a great challenge, not on God's part but definitely on yours. It is hard enough to deal with our genetic makeup without having to deal with other things we bring on ourselves by simply being in denial.

Resistance is a powerful tool used by that slithering snake God's warns us about, because as long as you are resistance the more you put in your pathway the longer your journey back to God becomes. Life feels stretched out like too little butter over to much bread. Your strength begins to hang by a thread in a gusting wind storm. The enemy knows the power in attacking your youth, destroying the mind is the same as damning the spirit that lives within. Some of us never get over the hurdles in life, and simply give up the fight by killing the voice inside that tried to help us in our weakest moments. The enemy knows the power of the mind and works very hard to gain that part of us. He cannot attack the spirit within us because it is pure and incorruptible, but he can attack our minds and gain possession over our spirit through it.

This attack from the enemy is to be taken incredibly serious due to its long term effects on your life. I believe his attempts to secure our minds are solely based on memories, suppressed emotions and lack of knowledge. When we are in a state of resistance all of these symptoms come into play but only Satan gains points in this game of life vs. death. Think to yourself right now; what exactly is going on inside your head? Probably a lot of memories, things of your past, people, and lessons learned and supposedly lessons unlearned. You could find lots of regrets there, all those shoulda's, coulda's, woulda's.

All those things Satan uses to make out a specific game plan design just for you. Trust me he is not playing the game of life and death without a strategic plan to ultimately destroy you. Now the real question here is what is your game plan or are you simply unprepared? No matter the answer to that question God is here to shine light on all uncertainty. Resist no more, accept the truth, and even if unbelief still hover, just know it is hovering over you but no longer has a place inside of you. By reading this book you are giving it an eviction notice, it must go! I would like to touch on the other source that the enemy feeds on.

He gets so excited about the women who allow a one track mind to get the better of them. When a one track mind is operating resistance is at its highest peak. It is dominating your life sending you down all kinds of pathways out of the will of God for your life. Can you say detour? The message He has placed inside of you gets more and more buried amongst the rebellion of your decisions to live life according to the standards of the world. What is a one track mind?

A one track mind operates on its own knowledge and understanding of life and all its data collected over the years of your life on Earth. A one track mind is very limited and cannot think beyond its limited knowledge or know how. It runs into many road blocks along the way of life, I mean many road blocks! Sometimes it just doesn't know what to do, whether it is something as simple as should you go left or right. A one track mind simply records data that is physical evidence it cannot go beyond an event or memories even a fantasy could rule it's decision making skills.

Women are constantly being ruled by this predator. Many of us are infected with it clever tactics as it invade our minds with its tainted vision, and limited resolutions. It is unable to fix or resolve any concerns, problems that may occur, nothing is completely done away with, just swept under the rug. It cannot and will not heal your broken heart it is designed to keep you in pain and anguish. Satan has design this particular process to look like stable thinking and the only true source of livelihood. The devil is a liar and he will not win, you can and will defeat his tactics through Christ Jesus, whom is part of God's game plan to free the mind of all mankind.

God states in His Word (see Ephesians) that the mind is to be renewed and transformed, God knows that our minds are so messed up and fill with junk that a transformation is needed. A transformation of the mind does not come over night, nor is it accomplish through any strength that we possess, only through our acceptance of the truth. Acceptance of the beginnings and how we got to this point in life does not have to be a mystery anymore. God has come to set the captive free, and by acknowledging you are indeed a captive can change your life forever. How about it? Would you like to be free? As with many of life's circumstances some people are affected more than others.

In this particular case where the one track mind is at work in the older women, who tends to be the harder ice to break, due to arrogance and pure stubbornness they are harder to reach and usher into a place of freedom. Older women have a keen sense of pride holding them captive to past learning leaving them stuck and unable to embrace God illuminations to His way. When a one track mind is active in an older woman she takes and guards all that was learned in her beginnings as precious jewels. Not realizing all that God has to offer is not to be in a box but should be exposed for all in her path to see.

Two things can happen when exposing all you have learned. Telling others can change their life or you can expose something that may not be necessarily true. You can confront and correct a wrong teaching or wrong interpretation of that teaching. You see when you go through life with all you feel God has given you as if it is a secret you are not shining light, you are keeping it in the dark. Nothing that God offers us is to be kept in the dark, for darkness cannot hold it anyway. It brightens the darkest closet it simply cannot or even tolerant being lock away it must and will be seen. Some older women walk through life with a false sense of accomplishment because they feel their wiser.

Yet, they have not gone pass their porch to save a lost soul. Spending all their days in a debate over who knows the scripture better or who has a better interpretation of what God is saying, and living their lives with no direction from God, just their own made up map of what salvation should be. They spend a lifetime in a church with a one track mind and a false sense of purpose. Looking down and tearing down any potential young person who is zealous and ready to share the Word of God outside the church walls. This tool of the enemy is utilize amongst many of the older saints, due to the limited thinking a false sense of power was developed as a result of this behavior. Causing the youth to inherit recklessness, and no direction. The resistance that we as a people have today has a source and Satan is not only to blame. Remember the mind has a purpose and that's to record data and keep all events pertaining to your life.

What events in your life took place that caused your resistance to God? I can definitely recall mine, I was a young girl surrounded by all these church goers who talk the talk and miss the walk. I witnessed all types of corruption. I always wanted to believe that every woman who danced in church and scream out to God loved and obeyed His will for her life. I had to learn a tough lesson of what may seem real isn't always so. I was quick to believe in what I saw in them to be true versus what was really in control of their behaviors.

Children are free spirits and we are not too play around with their innocence when it comes to matters of the mind and heart. Instead we should be on guard as to what they witness, and what is being recorded and stored as data in their minds. All these things will in fact become essential to how their resistance will come about. Resistance is being built as their knowledge of right and wrong develops. The mind holds all physical evidence all things done and undone so in our attempts to be perfect in front of the preacher, and the mothers of the church, pales in comparison to a child's life being corrupted with a double life. The resistance will build slowly but surely. I tried as a girl to seek out Christ to the best of my knowledge and what I ended up with was a lot of false impressions of what women in the church made Him out to be.

I felt they were my examples, my leaders, and I was to follow them. So in my attempt to find Christ I ran into some road blocks. The road blocks are caused by the one track mind. The mind that tells us this is what God wants and this is what having God should feel like. If you do not scream or dance this way you do not know or have Him in your heart. The one track mind could resemble an inherited trait passed on by your grandmother, mother or even a leader's influence in the church whom you have dedicated your time and trust.

A one track mind paralyzes you and hinders growth; it blocks the spirit of truth. It has an assignment to keep your eyes focus on people actions, how they look and create a false dependency on titles. The one track mind needs us to focus on what is being seen it cannot deceive us without the physical evidence; we are holding ourselves captive by not seeking out the truth. Something is wrong, we need to wake up! We are missing it; we are missing the spirit of truth by allowing ourselves to be control by a one track mind. Let's go a little deeper into the tactics of the one track mind that requires no correction, it needs no help, it has all the answers, it has its own interpretation of the Word and it knows exactly how to worship and preach. One thing for sure it is misleading, God does not operate through a one track mind.

The one track mind has its own identity, it has consumed yours. Any life force in this world not dependent on God is not of God. I do not know many who did not have to travel the pathway of false dependency on others to learn that in the end all we have is God, if the spirit of God does not abide in folk they cannot be trusted. Minds not govern or discipline by the Word of God falls prey to all manner of evil. You better believe that there is a rebel force that is in resistance to these powerful truths, what you must understand and decide is what side are you on, or even a better question, do you believe that there are any sides to choose from? How can we break free from this resistance? We can begin to break the chains of this deceitful foe by acknowledging the hold it has on us. Again a snapshot of yourself is require, you must review the evidence store in your mind, you must face a reality check, and more importantly you have to decide to see it and all it splendor, then begin to do something about it.

Remember, the one track mind is prepared for the self-check it knows how to hide from you so get your facts straight before attempting to expose, it will fight back. The one track mind has found a home in you and will not leave without a fight. Research is required, study the Word of God, you cannot face this reality alone you need God, remember you always need Him. To attempt to live this life without Him is suicide. Different events in my life crippled my ability to handle pain; I was unable to mourn the loss of a dear family member. I was told that I had to be strong for my family and not to cry, and show weakness. That adult injured me on the inside causing me to handle pain differently from the way it should be handled. She taught me how to suppress my emotions.

By suppressing my need to grieve I learned to hold in what should have been released. Therefore after and throughout life I begin to become unresponsive to hurts and disappointment. I begin to create reasons for people actions when they hurt me so I wouldn't have to deal with the pain. This was awful; it caused me to stay in an abusive relationship and then marriage for all the wrong reasons. I could not hear the voice of God in my life and was blind to his plan for me because I was too busy making excuses for people's actions so I did not have to hurt. It blinded me from what was happening and crippling my ability to react to the problem hindering my attempts to find a resolution. Suppressed emotion can kill you slowly. Let me take the time right now to thank God for his unchanging hands for without Him I would be a captive of my suppressed emotions. It is not the will of God that we hide our emotions, nothing hidden from the light of truth is good for you. It must be exposed; God sent his Son that light could be ushered in this dark Tween Place.

Allow His light to shine on your pain, let His light shine on your suppressed emotions. It is not His will for your life to be in darkness, stop trying to be strong. Allow God to be your strength, allow Him to be your example, and leader. Where does the need to have suppressed emotions come from, who planted that seed? God comes to set the captive free by freeing you He also frees up every single suppressed feeling you have locked away! It is vital to your humanity to get that mess out of you. Not only does it affect your health it destroys your ability to reach your supernatural side and receive your assignment.

Without your assignment the purpose of life leaves you and with that exit, what exactly is left? Do not remain a victim anymore learn the truth and search for it; I know you can find it! In a world where the very ground is curse, trust me you are not alone, you are with God. God has sent His Son that more like Christ could remain to help one another. Trust me there is more Christ like people out there, but how to find them? God will awaken in you the spirit of discernment and you will be able to find those individuals. God knows we need encouragement, this time, never forget whom your help cometh. Stop looking to man for what only God can give.

No matter what you have been taught, take it to God; test it against the Word of God to see if it can stand the spirit of truth. How many more disappointments will we continue to put in some type of perspective so we can continue living outside of God will for our lives? Remember the spirit of resistance creates excuses it will not be evicted without a fight; it needs you and all your suppressed memories to survive. Everything you have learned up to this point is aiding in its survival, you must sort through the mess, boot out what is false, embrace what is real and can stand in the light of God's Word.

When experiencing the reality of our life and denying its existence forces us into a resistance which leads us down thousands of pathways never leading to truth. Come with me to discover how the never ending journey down these forbidden roads ultimately leads to our defeat and death.

The Pathways

One day I was filled with such emotional pain about life's disappointments. My body was aching all over in a way that I have never felt before. I was overwhelmed with panic, followed by shortness of breath. I felt angry, fear, anxiety, and confusion. I had never felt so many emotions at one time possessing different meanings, feeling them altogether but still able to recognize each one separately. My heart was broken; I had no control over what was being done to me. How many of us think we are in control of our lives? What about that false sense of power, thinking we can control other people actions? What I was feeling that day was how out of control life gets and how out of control it made me.

Facing all those emotions was helping me to realize how out of sync I was with God. Life was just beating me over the head continually and all I could do was take it. I was fighting a losing battle with myself by throwing accusations at others for my pain. All of which was taking me down thousands of wrong pathways. These pathways were leading me straight to all the wrong answers, people, places, habits, you name it, and there is where you found me. Life is filled with tons of uncertainty and in this place where the double standard exists, nothing is guaranteed, everything is at risk, including your sanity. I reach out to God, asking, "Why is it that the people you love and trust the most hurt you?" In that same exact moment I heard the answer, "Insanity waits on the other side of revenge, let the seed of vengeance be cast away from your heart so that love may dwell there, when I speak of love I speak of myself said the Lord." God has given us the guidance to travel through the forest of life, we need only listen.

Listening sounds like one of those easy things to do, if that was true why are we so lost? God began to deal with me about pathways. Pathways are no different in meaning than a roadway or highway. We get into our cars or take a bus to get on the highway to travel it's the same when living out one's life through pathways. Pathways are simply choices we make throughout life. Pathways are extremely important and must never be taken lightly. This chapter will touch more in depth issues that will once again take us to the foundation in which we are building on, our true beginnings. Shall we start? How do pathways tie into the beginnings of life?

Remember how we discussed Adam's and Eve's beginnings, so is the same for us. Their decision created a pathway and we all know every pathway has a trail and an ending. Their choice to disobey God opened up the path to disobedience and consequence. Think back right now over your life, think on the choices you have made and pathways you have traveled. While living life you are indeed traveling, so if you are traveling on a pathway, where exactly are you going? What is your destination? Who is your travel guide? What are you using to direct you?

In life we use resources, collected data, visual aids, and so forth. Maybe you are piggy backing on someone else. Think about it….. where exactly are you? You are somewhere; you are using something to get to where ever you think you are going. One thing for sure, you are going to end up somewhere, but waiting to get there, only to ask where am I, will be a little too late, don't you think? Well not thinking about these very important points and ignoring your whereabouts will not free you from the end result. Let's face it now, we are lost. Yes, you are lost, and without the right guidance and direction from the one source who knows the beginnings and the end we are not going to survive.

Acknowledging first that you are in the Tween Place is the first step toward getting the guidance to finding out your whereabouts. We are living in the Tween Place to ignore its history leaves you vulnerable and hinders your ability to see clearly causing the inability to move forward. It brings fear causing you to be in a frozen state. Unable to function in a flow consistent to life's cycles of ups and downs. When paralyzed in this condition you continue to age, then life as you know it becomes a memory and no progress is ever made. Yes we are in a Tween Place, but thanks be to God we are not alone in this Place, we have a guide, His Holy Spirit has come to comfort us in this place (see Acts).

    The Holy Spirit brings the knowledge needed to empower us with the weapons to fight off the enemy, and directions to a place of shelter. When Jesus ascended to Heaven He left behind the Holy Spirit to be a light within us so that we may shine through the forest of darkness that others can see. We can show them the way to receiving the Holy Spirit. When in doubt seek out the light, walk toward the light. Look to the hills for which cometh your help, your help cometh from the Lord. God has sent His Son, and the Holy Spirit as a comforter. Our help is here we need only to seek it out. Think about your choices in life every single thing you do creates a pathway.

    You are constantly in motion, but are you moving forward, backwards, or are you simply traveling in circles? With so many decisions to make and the uncertainty of life echoing in the distance it's no surprise to me that so many of us simply stop moving forward in life. Life to me is like a giant forest, and upon approach fear of the unseen creeps over me. I began asking myself, what is in there? It looks dark, only a little light pierces the dark corners of the forest exposing me to more fear, giving a glimpse of wild life, insects, and a great possibility of getting lost.

    When focusing on the forest of life I see lots of distractions and things that could block my way and ensure my defeat. Just like life's influential people can hinder your growth, holding you back and causing you to waste time. It is very easy to get lost in the dark forest without the light. Piggybacking on someone else only gets you so far. The pathway of the person you are piggybacking on is a totally different path from that of your own, and all the while you felt you had made progress, you only became more lost, and was better off where you were. It is true, cheaters never win, so don't become one, and if you are piggybacking, jump off before they take you someplace you cannot return from.

Piggyback riding comes in many different forms. There are times when you don't know you're doing it. Co-dependency is a form of piggy back riding. Depending on someone else for your life support and guidance is a very dangerous behavior to have and could render deadly results. No one should have that kind of power over you, no one. Only God should be your life force in every life situation, only God! Let me break this down for you. We have leaders in this Tween Place chosen by God, whom we are to follow. God must dwell in the person leading and guiding as he leads you.

It is important that the relationship between you and God be constantly in motion while under the guidance of a leader. When I was a little girl I was attending church when the message of Christ was introduce to me. I accepted Jesus Christ as my Lord and Savior as a young girl in that church. My mother had decided that the pastor was her leader or guide through the forest of life and chose to follow him. She would consult him for any questions about her spiritual walk. In the forest I could imagine all the paths and trees that make every single thing look just alike. It's probably very easy to get lost, so I imagine one brave courageous person who shows no fear but feels fear, must still be able to lead standing in the front saying follow me I will get us to the other side.

In the same way the teachers and preachers who are called of God takes these same brave role of leadership. Leaders are constantly taking on full responsibility for the people who follow them ensuring a safe passage across unfamiliar territory. It is exactly the same case in the church, leadership is a necessity, but it is also a weapon that we have given to the enemy to destroy us with. Too many leaders have abused the power of influence in the church, using it to control people rather than to train leaders. Some leaders fail to grow more strong leaders based on their experiences and knowledge; they lock down any potential flourishing leaders in their church, selfishly keeping them to themselves in threat of being out done by their zeal.

Leaders are completely losing sight of God's great design for His body. Men who build empires to form civilizations still think they possess power over mankind. Placing it in a new form of authority the devil has out witted the church and now uses it to hinder true growth. God has leaders for a reason; leaders are to have a spirit of discernment, and the spirit of truth. Strength and fearlessness obtain through prayer and intercession directly to God, whom they refuel through daily. Receiving what is needed to give to those of less strength and knowledge. Leaders are to be continually seeking out direction from God for each new day.

Studying the Word of God becomes the life source; no longer will bread alone be enough, but the Word of God. No one man can handle the weight of the world; leaders are to develop more leaders and so forth. They ought to be better than their teachers avoiding the problems and challenging of their pastor whose teaching methods to aid in their spiritual survival. It is a long journey for some leaders, and waiting to the point of death to release one's mantle to the next leader is not the way. From one leader many should be developed and given assignments according to their gifts. Raised up to be strong in whatever they do unto God. Many are the gifts of mankind each one of us possessing different qualities, working together to the glory of the giver who is God. Your fate is not tied to your leader; it comes a time when you must depart to find who you are.

The introduction to Christ should be make known to the lost souls who crosses your path. You cannot stay with your leader forever. You have an individual destiny away from your leader. To raise new leaders to do exactly what was done for you, and nourish the gift within. Someone has to show them the way. Not to control, or gain power over them but to guide, we are not the judge or jury in the court of the Lord on the Day of Judgment. We are to assist in the discovery of mankind's true purpose and tell of how we uncovered the hidden truth of finding destiny. There are so many mysteries yet to be solved, so many lessons we still are in need of learning, who will lead us?

We cannot lead ourselves there is a higher power who see all, and know all. Think about it, we have our leaders in the church who have knowledge and who are gifted, but are they being led by God?

Our fate is not determined by man, but it is in the hands of the most High God, and he that follow not God should not be followed. Think back on your childhood for a moment, who was the person in your life whom you found your connection to Christ? Where are they now? What are they doing? Are the fruit of the spirit evident in their life? Did they give you a mantle of leadership according to your gifts? Did they even notice you had a gift? Many of us make the decision to stay in the same ministry for the duration of life, serving on the usher board, being a deacon, bringing the pastor his water, and are very pleased with doing so for years, and years with absolutely no progress, just as the body that you inhabit grows so must you. Everything in this world including you is in motion, time stops for no one. So why are you on pause, stating you are in God's will by being a true servant of the church, or my personal favorite "I am waiting on the Lord"? In everything we do in the body of Christ we do by faith, and faith without works is dead.

So if you are not stepping out on faith seeking out your assignment, you are not in motion. Therefore you are not exercising your rights to faith. Faith is how we trust God. Everything that revolves around the belief is based upon faith, so to not actively seek out destiny, is the same as not truly believing? How do you show you believe in something? Whether we want to admit it or not, those things we believe in we show by demonstrating a love for it, taking care of it, nourishing it, and fighting for it. How do we show God that we believe in Him, more than just saying it?

By obeying His Word, and putting your life in motion toward the Father. Accepting His Son Jesus Christ as your Lord and Savior is the very first step. Start the search in the forest of your life and begin to seek Him out. Deciding to accept the Son as your Savior will definitely change your path, but this time for the better. How did the decisions you made in the past affect your future? When you enter the body of Christ something very important happens to you, your eyes become open in a way that you have never used before. You begin to see things in a new light, therefore exposing the past behaviors and identities taken on.

All darkness that once consumed your body is now being forced out by the penetrating rays of light. That's when the trauma of the change feels like cardiac arrest. Spiritual awakening causes the body to feel deprived of its usual behaviors and desires. All though you are in pain and feel weaken, this is a good sign that your transformation is active and working a new creation in you. When I speak of pain I am speaking of emotional pain, feeling like you're being torn in two. When Christ enters us I believe it's not physical strength that we gain, but a spiritual awakening. A part of you will now begin to fight against the will of the Lord for your life. Your body, and mind with all its memories will begin to reject this move in.

With a goal to detour you back onto the pathways that only lead to dead ends. You must not allow this struggle between the spirit and flesh to take a hold of you. In these struggles you will learn to lean and depend on God, studying His Word to discover and learn of His Son Jesus. To know Jesus is to obey Him, to know how and what to obey you must first read the Word of God. Start your introduction to your new friend. Begin to form your new friendship with Him. Learn how to fellowship with Him. How can you lean and depend on someone you do not know?

To know Him is to love Him. Once you've had time to discover Him, than you can communicate with Him. The forest of life is filled with deceit, trickery, and manipulations. You must tread carefully and be led by God. When Jesus enters us He brings many gifts, I will name a few. He brings the gifts of sight, justification, purification, and transformation. These are just some of the few you receive in the beginning of your union with Him. These gifts will begin to manifest in your life. You need only to activate them. The way to activate these precious gifts is through the Word of God. He shows us exactly how to do this. Once the gifts begin to activate you are really in motion and it is very important that you stay that way.

Never should your time become idle, causing the enemy to catch up with you. Jesus is now an ever present presence in your life and is there for you by you choosing for Him to be there. He is not going to take over your body leaving you powerless to make your own choices, but He works through you and your invitation to have Him there. Being that our free will leaves us in a place of vulnerability we must make conscious efforts to stay in His will for our lives. Through His Word the guidance is always there. The forest of life must not be treaded through without this guidance and protection given to us through the Lord Jesus Christ. As we travel, being that every decision made is a pathway we must be certain that the decisions that we are making are being guided by Christ and not by us.

This is very important, due to the fact that now we can see through the forest and what we was once blinded to is now being revealed through Christ. He now lives within us, and as you travel the forest of life you can see in the darkest places because of the light that is now shining through your being. It makes you fully aware of all the hidden and dangerous things that the forest once hid from you. We meet a lot of interesting people in the forest, and when God was revealing to me the danger of meeting people in the forest I was in awe over how this trick of the enemy is played out and how quickly deceived I was to it. Before I accepted Jesus as Lord and Savior I walked in the darkness, and everyone was acceptable, as long as I had someone, I didn't really care who it was. In my desperate attempt to escape and leave the camp of sin to find a place of refuge, I found Jesus.

Now what about those I once lived amongst, what to do about them? Will I meet up with them again? Definitely! Those individuals are still traveling in circles and I am now moving forward. Excited to tell them what happened, some wanted what I discovered and others not so much, they even became violent in defense to their way of life. Seeing old friends will be part of your change, you may feel a bit scared considering you can see what you once lived amongst. That can be scary to see who you once were attracted to and fellowshipped with.

If your old acquaintances are no longer interested in you or your new found freedom, you must walk away and not spend a lot of time trying to convince them of what happened to you and how it can change them also. Once they begin to reject your light leave them and remember to keep them in your prayers. Just as Christ entered you, He will not enter them without an invitation to do so. Stay focus. As you continue on your path of righteousness you must be ready to handle what up ahead. Can you say "detours"?

Detours

Detours often occur when a powerful life changing decision has been made. Accepting Christ into your heart is life changing. Most often when the decision is made to accept Christ, the full understanding of that choice is not clear. We don't know exactly what to expect. We feel a sense of security in knowing life is about to get better, but we are not completely sure of anything. We can definitely agree that something just happened, and hope for life enters the heart. I learned a lot about detours from the beginnings of my choice to live for Christ.

What I feel I lacked was the understanding of my choice. Expecting some type of supernatural force to take over my life and live out my new found religion was reaching. When I look back on it, I find myself shocked at the thought of thinking Christ was going to take over my body and control me completely leaving my life flawlessly lived. I felt I needed to do nothing; I needed to decide on nothing, just be completely taken over to live life in a zombie like state of mind. Thankfully that assumption was quickly discovered to be untrue when life decided to test my new found salvation. The things that were hurting me and caused me to accept Christ in the first place were back and stronger than ever testing me to go against my decision to live a sin free life. There was no confusion about what I shouldn't do after accepting Christ because it was the things that were being done prior to that acceptance. Not to mention the nagging feeling in my stomach that warned me against it.

Detours are created in your life when the war on the inside starts. The war is between you and your decision to live life for Christ. You have an opponent, a very clever adversary; the devil himself. In the beginning of your new found faith your adversary is not so much the devil as it is you. You and your false assumptions and lack of knowledge behind this new found faith you have acquired. The bible tells us,

> That the path traveled by the righteous is straight and narrow, but broad is the path traveled by the evil doers.
> (Matthew 7:13)

There are no detours on the path that leads to righteousness. I believe that once we get off course and change pathways we enter into the unfamiliar territory of road blocks, detours, and horrible traffic. God require that we be focused and ever learning His will for our lives. This is the beginning of the journey through the Tween Place. You may be thinking I have lived many years and have been traveling, but before the decision to accept Christ you were not traveling at all just merely existing. The journey began when you chose to see and understand the purpose of mankind and the role you play in the battle between good and evil. When you are in the world merely living you have placed yourself in neutral. Choosing neither side places you on a path to self-destruction. You are no good for either side; you could not enjoy the satisfaction of victory or the sorrow of defeat. You lose the privilege to determine your fate. You freely give it to whomever to decide for you. A perfect example of this is a person who constantly is complaining about politics but refuses to vote. When you refuse to choose, you also lose the right to comment or complain. You lose the right to fight, why would you want to fight when you are loyal to no one. You believe in nothing just your unbelief.

Unbelief is a huge detour. Not truly believing in your choice to be in Christ set you up greatly to be detoured. When traveling the straight and narrow path doubt is the devil in his purest form of influence. Picture yourself headed north down a path, up ahead you notice a road block rerouting your path west. That road block is a perfect example of a challenge. When events in your day to day living are questionable against your new found salvation, a road block is actually a necessity to bring about self reflection. The straight and narrow path is one of certainty, doubt cannot dwell there.

Doubt happens when the inner struggle of what's really happening in your life ignites. A detour is what takes you away from your rightful path. It resets your path taking you the long way around versus that straight and shorter path. Detours are often tricks and manipulations placed in our path to take us off course. In the Word of God I found that when obstacles are set in my pathway to be a destructive force, God often turns these occasions into something better. Road blocks and detours come to hinder and confuse, but at the same time they bring clarity, and reflection. Let's discuss some of the offspring's delivered from detours. Reasonable doubt set in when allowing thoughts of the past to enter your mind. Sometimes we are unable to control the large amounts of corrupt thinking that plagues our daily living.

When we neglect to make conscience effort to fill our minds with new found knowledge of life which is found in the Word of God we are agreeing to keep the old way and the new filth that is to come. The bible teaches us how to cleanse our mind and how important it is for it to be transformed (see Ephesians). The mind must be renewed with the Word of God. The Word of God equips the mind with the power to wage war against anything that's not like Christ. Doubt is not like Christ, so if it exist in your mind than its existence will dwell in your heart. A road block is definitely necessary. You are off course a stop needs to be made to get you on track again.

Doubt must be fought against it cannot be something you ignore. To ignore it gives it permission to operate in your life, hindering the growth of righteousness and its fruits. Don't allow doubt to ruin the productivity of Christ entrance into your life. Many complain about not seeing the fruitfulness of Christ in their lives, but if you have the seed of doubt in your garden its very presence in your life will hinder the growth of Christ. It must be up rooted immediately! You may ask how, I will tell you how, there is only one way, and that is through the Word of God.

Another way to get into a traffic jam is by letting outsiders influence your decision making. Why is it that we listen to the advice of others who have no idea of what we are going through? When we enter into the body of Christ many things in our life we have to change, and one of those changes are the company we keep and who we decide to take advice from. You cannot listen to the home girl you once club with when it comes to the struggles of your new Christian walk. What in the world would she know about the tactics of the enemy or your inner struggles?

I'm not saying throw your friend away, but get strong in your walk with Christ pull all the doubt out of your heart so you can help her. Until then, seek out help from those who can relate to your struggles, speak with your pastor or another sister in Christ, but not the friend who is still in sin. Remember you are still very weak and need training, so listening to the wrong people is a sure way to get thrown off course. Many are the lessons to be learned when on the path to righteousness, no one is perfect, striving to be; should be the goal. Purposely falling into sin is unacceptable.

When learning the lessons that help to make you stronger and wiser will feel a bit overwhelming at times, but you must not lose hope. These lessons are building your character, strengthening you so when someone crosses your path and need your help you can speak to them from a place of experience and not from something you just over heard but know nothing about. Your experience gives the testimony; its life changing power was drawn from a place of belief and that belief of Christ.

It's all from Christ. When you believed you were freed and with that freedom you experienced the power of God. In witnessing the power of God you know beyond logic and reason that He is indeed real. Now you are truly able to speak from a place of power and strength to deliver someone else from their darkness as you travel along your pathway. Logic and reason goes out the window when Christ enters. In order to make the first step in God you must first believe in what you cannot see. This is what we call faith (Hebrews 11:1-2). Faith is being sure of what we hope for and certain of what we cannot see. As we continue to believe in God, He is faithful in revealing Himself. Only God has the power to reveal that which is made invisible to the world. He sets in place the steps needed to find Him. He is just in His approach to capture our hearts.

He made the first move, He loved us first, and He sent His Son, now He waits for us to invite Him in. Jesus Christ will never enter by force, always gentle and with love. Who can resist such a loving invitation? I can't. How about you? We have absolutely nothing to lose, but everything to gain. Logic and reason are signs that doubt exist in your heart. Logic and reason comes when not enough Word is in you. You are not reading it, or hearing it. You are simply pondering the gossip of men who chose to debate over it by putting it in some type of universal science.

The world cannot ration the things of God they are indeed supernatural the human brain cannot understand it. This is why you need the spirit of God within you to reveal the mysteries of His Word. A perfect example of this is when a sinner is introduce to Christ and have accepted Him into their heart, but never goes to church, never read the bible; no training of any kind is received. When she goes out to face the world logic and reason becomes her best friends and she believe that she was just feeling bad and the church made her feel like she needed Christ but she no longer feels the same. She has stepped back into the world unprepared and the world is ready to steal her precious gift of salvation. She is extremely vulnerable; she's a babe in Christ and is in need of great protection. The world will always attack a faith base religion with logic and reason, one of their best weapons toward a babe in Christ. What I'm trying to relay is you must stay faithful in your walk with Christ. Stick close to mature saints, stay in your Word. So that when logic and reason rears its ugly head you can resist its tactics.

SELF-JUSTIFICATIONS

After experiencing all those road blocks, detours, and traffic jams you may wonder how is life on the other side. Well for me, life changed a lot; I went straight into self-justification mode, not at all a good place to be. I took some of those detours it seemed over and over and over again, because I was just not getting it. I did not understand the purpose behind it. I felt I was just having an unfortunate case of bad luck. It seemed every decision I was making was throwing me into depression and resentment. I became a very angry person. I was constantly in rage mode, blaming anything and everybody for what was happening to me.

Life was trying to teach me something and I was not at all interested in what those lessons were. I always felt like I had it all figured out, little did I know with that attitude I was headed straight for self-destruction. On your way to self-destruction you'll meet up with a new friend call self-justification first. This is not a friend you would like to hold on to. Trust me. Remember, where she is leading you to. When experiencing the detours in a particular season in your life, you are sometimes left with tons of negative feelings.

You have positive feelings but they become smothered under the negativity. The reason behind the smothering of your positives is your mind set, and its inability to comprehend the righteous outlook of those lessons. The mind that is not yet been transformed by the Word of God cannot see the lessons in bad situations. Its only focus is the bad; the mind is using logic and reason to determine its reaction and future move. So now you're placing the decision on what to do next on your limited experience, and tainted vision. You are now relying on yourself to provide answers and to reveal understanding of exactly what is happening to you and why?

So what you just got out of all that turmoil was a very negative boost of self-assurance. I really want to deal with how bad we are and how we get in the way of God's plan for our lives. As I stated in the previous chapter, in the beginnings of our acceptance to Christ, the enemy is the leased of our worries. The very thing we should be consumed with is the hidden villain we know as "Self". No one wants to be the blame of their pitfalls, detours, and roadblocks. The way we view the obstacles in life is the key in overcoming them. Self-justification is one of those hardest behaviors to explain, due to the fact that it's always viewed as self-esteem.

The way to discovering if your life is plagued by its fruits is to unveil its disguise. Let's first discuss what it looks, and sounds like. You would think it's beautiful, maybe even glamorous. In all actuality, it is quite the opposite, it looks worn out, and as if life is sucking you dry. Self-justification leaves you with such a huge appetite for fulfillment, and an endless black hole of unsatisfied experiences and relationships. You are unable to give or receive love. You wouldn't recognize a great thing even if it hit you right on the head. It blinds you to the beauty of life, and deafens you to the sound of it. The very essence of joy, you could not experience, but not without lack of trying. You carry around a defeated attitude even when attempting to hide it.

Self-justification has to be exposed and dealt with diligently and without hesitation. Think about yourself for just one moment…what are you like? Sometimes we cannot truthfully answer that question, because we cannot see ourselves clearly. Remember you are the pilot who is flying the plane of Self-justification. There is a serious need for someone else to look at you from a prospective that you cannot see. This individual cannot just be anyone but someone who has your spiritual success at heart, and loves you beyond the point of hurting your feelings. Truth can be a very hard subject to tackle but with the

help of the Lord Jesus Christ it would be most welcomed. Truth is like an ongoing pouring of rain from the Heavens that seems as if it will never stop, but when it does it has supply you with plenty for every seed planted to flourish, and enough water to purify your soul. So in other words… let it rain! Allowing the floods gate to open is a totally different issue, some would prefer to stay in the dry places of the desert, but those looking to find the oasis, follow me. Open the gate and release the river of purification. Expose your way of thinking, speaking, and living. By exposing these very things you are taking full steps ahead to revealing the hidden behavior of self-justification. Thinking, your mind set, what is it like, and why it needs to change.

Who can help you with the way you think if you never expose your thought patterns. In any given situation in life we are always definitely thinking on what, how, when, where, and why. So if everything about who we are is surrounded by a thought pattern how can we get ourselves to think correctly or should I say, in a way that will bring true fulfillment and purpose in our lives. So, the real question is, how do we get there? We must first understand that everything we surround ourselves with every day is becoming a part of us. Those things we spend the most time doing are the very things we are falling in love with.

Whether we choose to acknowledge it or not it is becoming a part of you and the way you think. So, what are you thinking about? Example, if I sit around thinking about how I wish I was a millionaire, do you think I will actually become one. Some might say "yes", because it all you seemed to think on, but that's not true. When self-justification is within you, the way things are viewed are somewhat twisted. Sitting around thinking on becoming a millionaire will get me no closer to wealth than drawing a picture of it. Why is this? It is because when self –justification exists within it will not allow you to believe what you are dreaming, or fantasying about.

Self-justification will not allow you to see the works in achieving wealth just the end results. When this behavior exists within you there is no follow through just a lot of idle thinking and wishing. It will smother your ambitions with false hope, and sinks you into a pool of self-doubt. It will block the seeds of inspiration that try to flourish with each new day, and ignore great advice with its double minded thinking. It will make you proud and give off a false sense of pride, creating an illusion of self–awareness and an attitude of isolation.

Self-justification needs to keep you away from anything and everyone who could possibly play a role in your life, changing it for the better. It always wants you to feel that you need no one, that you can do it alone. It wants to be the only voice you rely on. Self-justification becomes the only source of strength when life gets too hard. This is a setup and a straight path to self-destruction. I know this is a lot to swallow, but remember when it rains it pours. Selfjustification manifests itself in another form of thinking, the way we handle our emotions. When things in life hurt us, we choose to keep them, no matter how painful they are, we make excuses for them.

Example, when in a bad relationship self –justification causes us to believe that it is ourselves that is doing something wrong or we are simply not good enough. When in a relationship with a man and he's cheating and you're taking care of home, and family and he simply decide to be with someone else, the pain alone is unbearable. Selfjustification instantly gives off an illusion that we deserved it because we didn't do something or look a certain way. This is a manipulative trick of the mind when self-justification exists, if only we could expose this dangerous behavior for what it is, in the light of His Holy Word.

Then we can be freed of it, no longer calling it self-esteem, but self-destruction. It took me a very long time to come to these powerful truths, don't allow such a waste of time to happen to you. Live now in the abundance of truth, to feel, hear, see, and breathe in all its blessings their waiting for you! The way we think has such a huge impact on everything we do it truly blew me away. When I remained sleep to negative and powerless thought patterns, every single day I lost the battle with life because of my thinking. Living life in a defeated bubble was the worst and most frustrating prison that existed. All because I could not see it, it was invisible to me.

Self-justification blinds you to the cage in which you live in due to the way you think. The only way to freedom is to find the key and the key is in the Word of God, waiting to free you, just waiting. SelfJustification causes you to live life so selfishly; it's all about you, all the time. You will do nothing unless it pleases you. Seeking praise in everything you do, if none is received than you regret doing it. In your heart you selfishly wish to take it back, your hands are always closed and never seeing the good in anything or anyone, just yourself. Fixing situations to glorify yourself, and everything is always about personal gain. You look to the world for your reward and complain if none is received.

This very self-destructive behavior leads you to a place of great danger, but who will help you, when you have allowed everyone who cared about you to be pushed away. Who will hear your call for help when you realize how much trouble you're in? Never forget the pathways and the place it's leading you to. Don't wait, do something about it, fight now, challenge it, make it reveal itself, so that it can be dealt with according to the Word of the Lord. Self-justification works on the mind daily telling it "to do whatever it takes to get ahead". It carry a take no prisoners type attitude.

Step on the little man, leave the slow behind, ignore the poor, take what isn't your, I got to think of myself first, I did this, I did that, never giving the glory to anyone, but always expecting the glory. The voice of self-justification, always justifying its actions no matter if they are dead wrong, it feels right. It will make it right even if manipulation is necessary it will be justified. Only the Word of God can bring the illuminating light on this behavior to expose and set free it's captives. Self-justification never allows you to accept responsibility for your actions. It actually helps you in making excuses and even aids in your complete denial of doing anything wrong.

Unable to recognize right or wrong, everything becomes gain or so you are tricked into believing that your actions has no consequences. Self-justification lacks conscience therefore it is easy to fall into these evil acts of heartlessness for human life. It has no respect for anyone, and cannot be trusted. Self-justification always causes its victims to become paranoid and overly caution. This is all part of the plan, a trick, entrapment, and the constant need for isolation. When you are alone it's easier to be influenced, and maintain control of your life, keeping you in a self –destructive pattern.

Self-justification is only one of the many weapons the enemy uses against us, but this one he allows us to hold. Self-justification waits for the behavior to mature, and become strong holds in our lives, than he joins in with self-inflicted torment when the consequences are ready to be harvested. He uses all the consequences of your actions to beat you over the head with. Using your guilt, to make depression, and regret to sow hatred into your life. Now you're walking around saying no one loves you, and that you're all alone, then the blame game starts. Self-justification will need to be removed from your life. Allowing it to stay is an invitation for growth into a stronger form of deceit.

Its tactics and plans for you will only become more aggressive and ruthless. The final plan for you on the watch board of the enemy is self-destruction. The enemy knows one of the greatest sins is for man to take his own life. The enemy ultimate goal is to make us self-destruct. Now we are dealing with another sign on the pathways showing a "wrong turn" of self –inflicted punishment. Believing we don't deserve anything good to happen to us, punishing ourselves for bad choices, and unable to move forward because we're stuck in the past. You cannot undo what has already been done, but you can be redeemed, if you only ask. This is all a part of learning what it truly means to accept Christ into your heart.

You need to understand the why, and what's at stake if you don't understand how not accepting this precious gift affects you. I'm just too curious of a person not to weigh all my options in life, especially those made clear to me. Those options came to me for a reason; I was destined to hear the invitation to Christ, just as you were destine to read this book. Nothing in life is a coincidence, everything has a purpose. Just as self-inflicted punishment was a road way sign along the pathway of life, so is the breakdown of your moral character a huge red and white stop sign. The enemy wants you to lose your mind, knowing that breakdown could insure him your soul.

It is of the upmost importance to keep your mind right. Keeping your mind right, so it may take the journey of transformation with God's Holy Word. You must take care of your mind. For once you begin to expose those destructive forces in your life you must hold on to your sanity. Your training will soon begin; this is why once the decision to enter the body of Christ is made you need to remain amongst the strong. The strong in Christ will protect you from the ways of the enemy. On the path to destruction the loss of confidence appears as a "yellow light". When choosing to serve the Lord people of all kind will surface. Some God has placed in your path to help you along the way, and other planted by the enemy himself. You must begin to saturate yourself with the Word of God. That you may be able to see the road signs. In this case, being blinded to who people really are would be a "danger ahead" sign.

The strong saints can see what you are still blinded to, and assist you on your new found sense of direction. One thing I remember in my struggle to come out of self –justification was the feeling that I had loss all confidence in myself. When in all actuality I never had confidence I was being control by a spirit assigned to destroy me. Anything you felt you gain while in the world living by it rules, forget about it. When you cross over to Christ you can't bring those things along. They were conceived in darkness and cannot survive in the light.

They were never truly yours, but what God has in store for you, those things are truly who you are. They produce the essence of life itself, and the harvest of greatness that will be shared with the world. Becoming who you are meant to be is awesome; it is an incredible journey that is worth fighting for. Now as you empty out all that's not like God allow Him to fill in all the voids.

The Void

Productivity does not exist in this realm of life. Peace is just a mere thought, a daydream. Everyday life feels unbearable. Everything is an extreme; life feels like an endless circle leading to nowhere, a pointless journey you never signed up for anyways. Seeking absolution is like a job you long to quit, a lottery you will never win, a mansion you would love to own. Life's biggest fantasies, floods your mind daily. The void is a state of emptiness, an unquenchable thirst for better living, an unfulfilled craving for a perfect love, and the desperation to fix all that is broken.

The void evolves into a power struggle that forms inside you battling between who you are and who you are to become. This power struggle erupts inside you like a volcano; causing the pressure to control everyone and everything, even fate. As I began to write this chapter, I became so troubled by how to explain such an intense part of life. It is a very sensitive topic for many. I have experienced panic attacks about what I felt helpless to control. Other people in general gave me many sleepless nights. I would like to touch on these sensitive places in our lives, were we feel most vulnerable. The vulnerable places inside of us form the foundations were the voids are rooted, in these empty unfulfilled places in our hearts leading to the lack of understanding in our minds; feeding this bottomless place.

To better understand why these places exist is one step closer to becoming whole. Dealing with these tender areas of the heart takes courage that originates from strength beyond human reach. It comes from a different place, beyond the knowledge that education in scientific things provide. It's more than a degree from higher learning, its divine awakening. Divine awakening awaits your request for activation that it may provide you with all the knowledge and power necessary for your transformation. The voids in my life threaten every single thing God had for me.

It threaten my very sanity, crushing my self-esteem, and purpose for existing. It caused me great distress and constant hardship. I became a slave to high imagination, always in a dream world, never facing my realities. Not being able to see myself clearly, caused me to always be in search of someone to fill me up, with their time and attention. When I didn't receive these things, the void grew bigger and deeper inside of me, causing all kinds of symptoms. Depression grew inside, as well as repression. Obsession was also there causing addictions to form.

Obsession drove me to enter into premature relationships; forming false expectations of others and becoming angry when revealing who they were. Suppression helped me ignore my hurts and let downs, rooting myself in denial. Feeding myself false assurances to ignore the heartaches, which caused them to go deeper and widen the void within. Repression caused me to create excuses for others when they hurt me, and to keep secret my true feelings when I felt I had been wronged by someone. I became a passive aggressive person, who agreed with everything even when I didn't agree.

The offspring of such behaviors produce empty desires and unfulfilled hopes causing traits promoting self-destructive personalities, and attempts to kill not only me but my destiny. I want to speak in general of the danger of the voids within us, but I cannot explain it without making it personal. It was very real for me as I believe it is for many. Out of all the things I bring to your attention this could be probably one of the most serious I want badly for you to embrace. The voids within us, has the ability to kill us. To destroy and eliminate, is the main objective.

We must move swiftly to prevent such a hostile takeover. It cannot be ignored; we must begin to seek out the truth no longer allowing the void to grow consuming our lives and destroying our destiny. I began to notice everything in life shares a hidden connection. When blinded to who you are that connection is hidden from you. When you are unable to put together, the up's and down's, and see the lessons in the storm you are in a void. There are so many lessons we are to learn, just as if you were in school learning and not paying attention, you would miss it.

Life is just like that, you must pay attention to what your life experiences are trying to teach you. It's a bit complicated but I will do my best to describe what I mean. For example, you can be experiencing financial hardships. The true reasons these hardships exist are because you're a compulsive shopper. The true color you should see for your money problems will be the color red. When seeing and experiencing these hardships you always seem to see a different color. Let's say the color blue is denial. In this particular situation your reality is that you spend money like drinking water, but whenever you experience a financial hardship you never see the true color in it, you see the color blue not red.

Never accepting responsibility for what is happening with your finances leaves you blinded to a solution. Without acknowledging we have a problem is a sure way of staying in it. The void continues to grow while we are stuck in denial, like oxygen to a small fire. The void is fueled by so many things; I will focus on the more damaging aspects of it. One of the most important lessons I had to learn in life is to know I cannot control others, I can only control myself. It should never be your focus to change or control another person. Your motive should always be centered in love, not personal gain.

The value of your efforts should promote life in another, not destroy their self-esteem or seek out power over them. Never should your intentions be to prey on the weak, that you may look strong. There are so many way to help you understand this vital point, bear with me as I attempt to uncover your eyes and open your heart to the endless possibilities of walking through life with your eyes wide open.

Eyes wide open? Now what does that mean exactly? Hopefully by the end of this chapter that answer will be revealed. I have revealed some of the effects the void renders, but maybe I can shine light on how it originates.

Voids don't start out so noticeable, more like little disappointments, and let downs. Not the kind of disappointments we experience as adults, but the ones we suffer during our childhood the times when our personalities are being shaped. Many fail to realize the huge significant of our childhood experiences. The childhood years are the very foundation we build our life upon. It is everything and influences many major decisions made in the future. Trying to fill the voids in our lives are extremely difficult without uncovering the hurtful experiences of our past. There is a process in everything that brings true freedom.

The uncovering of misunderstood situations and damaging wounds incurred doing our childhood, cannot be faced lightly. When uncovering the dark places in life you need the light. Why uncover what you cannot see? The light in a situation is simply the understanding. The Word of God brings the illumination needed to face the dark places of ignorance. There are many ways the soul leads us to handle the why's in our life, and then their God's way. God's way is simple. There are not a million different directions its only one. We can't continue to walk down a million pathways to the point of exhaustion. We can choose to go straight and face all that is needed to fill the voids, by simply going straight and through, the narrow path.

I found that as I chose to go straight and through life it became a bit uncomfortable. I was use to the predictable burden of my past and became frustrated with traveling that circle. I begin to see how making what I thought was safe choices were the crippling effects that left me unable to succeed at anything I touched. Fear leaves you completely disabled, lame as a horse, and abandoned. Isolation is denial best friend, now becoming a part of your daily living. When isolated this spirit has the power to influence your life more, without the nagging concerns and comments of family and friends, or other influential persons in your life. The spirit of isolation gains its power by keeping you in a state of solitude; with no interference from others it works hard to consume you.

Secretly feeding your mind, creating false assumption of others, aiding you on with false excuses to justify failures, and accusations of why you're not succeeding in life; teaching you how to play the blame game. All the while no one enters into your world, the spirit of isolation is always their whispering, taking you deeper into the void. Its ultimate goal was there to destroy me in my very own emptiness. The spirit of isolation gave me a false impression of safety. It made me feel like I was safe, secure, and stable. It constantly spoke to my mind saying "you're better alone, no one can hurt you now". In that false impression it took away my need to seek out my purpose and took away my need to survive but brought in a complacent mind set. In this complacent mind set I lacked drive and my will to find purpose evaporated. I no longer sought out my purpose. I no longer wanted to discover my destiny. I became numb, stuck in a zombie like state of mind. God has that freedom, and waits for us to acknowledge Him. God is not a wizard that makes any of life dilemmas magically disappear. He takes every bit of what we go through and turns it for our good and uses it to strengthen us.

God gives us the power to defeat the suppressing spirits and strong holds that imprison our minds. He who the Son sets free is free indeed….don't you want to be free? You have to want it more than anything, but to want it, you have to understand it. That takes us back to the light, the illuminating power of God's Word bringing understanding to the most trivial things. God makes all the confusing, complicated situations simple. When you find yourself seeking after many answers you're feeling lost. To be found is simple, go to the source and become powered by the light of God. When thinking on life and the decisions we make, it puts me in mind of a dark room.

No matter how big or small it still remains dark. The size is irrelevant. Think about it, when you have a problem does it matter how big or little it is when there is no way out of it. You are blinded to a solution. When you cannot see, everything is bigger, higher, and harder. You are unable to judge the precise direction you are to head in because you are unable to see. That's how the void operates in your life it blinds you to all that moves. It takes the smallest of things and betrays them to be huge mountains, and provoking false dependency on people that don't have your best interest at heart. The void is a very delicate and serious issue to touch on, and almost impossible to make absolutely clear.

There are so many directions in which its takes you, but as I continue to go deeper, stay with me. Here are some additional points concerning the voids inside that we must face, we must become aware of the life cycles we travel. Remember earlier in the chapter I spoke of how your upbringing is vital to the way you handle your life when you have yet to be expose to the light. Once you reach a certain age the awareness of right and wrong come into play. Not so much because of the instructions you receive from those in charge of your care, but when the little voice within starts to touch your consciousness alerting you of good and bad behaviors.

I believe we are all born with a presence of good inside, that even when not instructed by an adult, we can sense the right thing to do, because there is good within; preordained goodness. Now having the power to choose to listen to that feeling is a whole different subject. I think that's when discipline comes into play.

This discipline is attained by the guardians of our mortal lives. These persons can be a mother, father, aunt, uncle, teacher or preacher. It could also be all these people together, writing and imprinting on your life. Wow, what a lot of different personalities flowing inside your fresh young mind.

It's no wonder we have problem figuring out who we really are, because we have had so many influential people in our lives, telling us what to do and how to be. It's no longer a surprise to me that I struggled to find out why I sometimes felt like more than one person; due to the many people who had written on the blank pages of my life. Debating the straight and narrow path is a way to initiate the frozen state. You are not moving forward or backwards, you're just stuck in a nothing; aging but not progressing. Being in a frozen state is deadly in every kind of way. You become vulnerable to every manipulating trick the force of darkness releases; you are a sitting duck. When voids exist in your life becoming frozen is just a part of the cycle it takes you through.

Always remember, the life cycle you go through when voids are present, it's almost like being in rotation. Insanity knocks at the door of your soul daily. How long will it take before you answer? Ways to detect the frozen state of your life is when you struggle to forgive others, to love, or receive love, always dreaming, unable to keep your mind from wondering, wishing for unrealistic goals, and neediness. Women struggle endlessly with idealizing their lives, especially when they favor a man. We will see him, date him, marry him, and have his child before we even say hello. Then wonder why he turns out to be an abuser, and cheat. The reality is he always was an abuser and a cheat. We simply created an alternate reality with him to fill the need created by the voids.

Not giving ourselves a realistic chance to even get to know who he is before creating who we wanted him to be. This is a perfect example of how the void operates. Whatever inside that you lack, the void will seek it out in others even if that means creating false realities. It will do whatever it takes to be fulfilled. Special care must be given to these extremely sensitive places that we may not fill them with the wrong stuff. Consequently nothing that enters the voids will stick anyway. It will only pass through, it makes you realize why you are always going through and afterward left completely empty.

Only that which is meant to stay will last, everything else falls straight through. Only the filler that lies in the hand of the Creator will sustain your life and make it complete. I'm not telling you something I've only heard but what I've lived. Let's travel to those empty places inside you right now, think on them, what do you see? I once struggled so greatly to love and receive love. I loved for all the wrong reason. I loved with the expectation to be loved back in the same way. No one will love the way you love. You are special and one of a kind, stop expecting a mirror image love to come back to you. You love because you chose to, not for any other reason; don't put a price on your love. Allow it to remain selfless and look to Heaven to fill your heart. Loving with unrealistic expectations of another isn't love at all. That's called quid-pro-quo. Loving someone because of what they own, or how they look, tell me; how long do you expect it to last? God's teaches us how to love through His Word, and when we put what He says to work, guess what? It produces more love and happiness beyond any life expectations. Try it. Learn to ask God to increase your love, not in just some areas but in all things. Learn to follow your inner voice, and to trust it.]

Learn to love and give unconditionally, and wait for it to return to you from the ultimate giver of life, God. All of this and much more can be accomplished through the light that is needed to usher in the waters of understanding, be filled with them. I believe in the connection of marriage God desires us to share as one, but yet I feel the core has not been touch. This is due to all the junk that exist between two totally different individual governed by an unyielding spirit to change. Please don't tell me, you enter into marriage and expect not to be altered in anyway. Remember those false expectations of what it takes to become one with another, we enter into a real situation living a dream, and then awake angry and frustrated with no one to blame but ourselves.

The void wants to suck the life out of life, and when you give yourself over to it, everything you bring into your life that breathes will be taken, and ultimately you. The void creates great distress, not only does it freezes our spirituality, and emotional asset; it causes us to fall short in everything we do. We have great ideas that we can never see through, leaving a welcome mat for self –doubt. You see how it progresses; the void grows and grows until it has consumed everything. You must not allow it to take you. Seek out the light and summon the life changing illuminating power of God, found in His Holy Word.

There are many ways to travel in life, endless choices, but which way to go? We can move forward to face uncertainty, we could go backward, were life is predictable, or stand still, to live in fear. Moving forward for me was just as scary as standing still. Moving forward in life caused me to be afraid when I looked at it incorrectly. Being able to understand the possibilities open to me when attempting a fresh start was the key in opening the door to success. Attempting to go forward without the vital part of life can be scary; I had to discover that vital part missing from my life. My mind would be stuck in wonder trying to figure out the test of Time.

I would sit for days just debating how Time works, envying it. I envied Time; it always seemed to keep moving no matter what was happening in the world, it never stops. I started to realize and see Time as an entity, not just a mere thing, but a presence. No matter how painful a loss or devastating a storm that destroys everything we build in this world Time keeps moving forward. Thinking on it reminds me of an aunt I lost at a very early age, I sure did love her, and she was taken in a tragic car accident, losses like this makes you feel like Time has stop moving, but again it does not, not even for the worst tragedies.

In this world we have seen so many tragedies and learned of the ones we have not witnessed, all the same, Time keeps moving forward. What are the lessons from Time we are to learn? It's amazing to me, how we are surrounded by this lesson every single day, yet blinded to acknowledging it as our teacher. Time wants to teach us how the voids in life are the cause of not learning the lessons. I'm always so slow to start anything that I feel lead to do, and it's a reason for that delay. I can always see myself accomplishing the things in life I want to do, but never was able to even tap the surface.

I began to give myself a personal examination to get to the source of my procrastinations and discovered my lesson from Time. My curiosity to understand Time showed me the voids in my life. It helped me to see how voids are hindrances. I begin to envision a large field of grass as far as the eye could see, I was standing at the beginning of the field looking over it, imagining how great it would be to cross.

It looked simple to just walk across, when I look harder I noticed everything in life I longed to have, do, and become. I was excited and begin to move forward full of expectation, hope, pride, and ready to embrace all that was for me. Then suddenly, I fell into a small hole, very shallow, just wide enough for me to trip over and fall. I got up, shook it off and thought; where did that come from? Dusting myself off thinking that was odd such a little hole, how come I didn't see that? In life as we move forward with Time we will experience small unforeseen holes, voids.

Already put into place and some we help create. Just as God has put Time into place, so has your life lessons been placed in your pathways in an effort to help you discover your true self. You will need to go through some things already placed in your path to help you. That reminds me of a friend who wanted to become a security guard at a prison facility. She began her training, when approached with a final lesson. She had to learn what it meant to use her pepper spray. You may be thinking well who needs training on how to hold and spray a can of spray? Anything that can affect the health and well-being of others needs to have a lesson taught to understand the value and responsibility. She needed to understand the importance of when and how to use this new weapon.

So, in the training her instructors spray her with it, and it hurt badly, beyond her expectations, she said it was extremely painful causing a shortness of breath, burning not only her eyes, but her skin as well. In all the symptoms she felt, what bothered her most was how helpless she felt against it. Then she tells me, I never want to experience that again, nor will I ever want to have to do it to someone else. With her face burned all around her eyes, I looked at her, and said, you see; you learn the lesson in it all. Many of us experience life lessons every day and just don't get it, ultimately creating more voids to fall into when crossing the field of your life.

Once you fall you wonder as I did, where did this hole come from? When you have fallen into enough holes in life, you become afraid to move forward. Not realizing, Time wants you to face your reality. Your life becomes an unpredictable mine field of holes and uncertainty, you become stuck, and afraid of risk. All the while you're standing there, and our teacher, Time does not wait for you, he continues to move forward. Time in this instance feels like the enemy, aging you and creating a depressing and defeated life. Don't allow life to make you feel like Time is the enemy because he is not. Time is your friend when embracing your destiny.

Learn the lesson Time is offering to you. My friend wanted that position bad enough to risk the uncertainty of being sprayed with a toxic chemical, not knowing how her body would react to it, she could have walked away, but instead chose to face up to it, and become who she was to be. Now, if the opportunity ever arise that would cause her to use her weapon she knows the effects and would use it only if necessary, never taking it for granted, or acting out of ignorance. What would the world be like if in order to own or use a gun you had to be shot first, how many gun handlers would we have then, not many?

Time wants us to pay attention to its voice in our life; it has been here since the beginning and will continue to exist long after were gone. I would think it is better we learned from it instead of fighting its purpose for teaching us. We need Time, because in Time we learn our reasons for being, everything in Time learns its purpose. What I refused to accept years ago I have learned to accept now; the lessons I fought against have changed my life for the better. Stop fighting against Time learn those lessons and make Time your friend, just as the fruit of a tree, and flowers of the field, allow Time to expose who you truly are to be. As Time continues to mature me and allow the world to see my beauty I realized that, Time is also quite divine. Time is God, the ultimate educator of life. He is to be feared, reverenced, honored, glorified, and more importantly embraced. Time is all around us; He is in everything and lives amongst everybody, everywhere all the time. Just as Time moves forward again we must also, but not in ignorance, and in false hope, but we must move forward in the illuminating lessons of Time.

Allow Him to illuminate your path, to prepare you for the voids you cannot foresee ahead. This is the key point I'm speaking, you are going to age whether you want to or not. Time will continue to move forward whether you want it to or not, it cannot wait for you. No one with all his money and power can stop it, it is beyond human reach, and it is indeed supernatural. So how do you become a student of its divine knowledge and power? You must first acknowledge its existence. The attack in this life that causes us to fall usually forces us to seek out better ways to walk.

In your search for a better life you will stumble upon Time, and He will show you the way, hopefully you will be ready to listen. A mentor once told me that listening is a skill, I think he's right. Not everybody has the skill of listening. Just like many will read this book but not everyone will receive its lessons. There is another seduction at work in our lives; can you hear it? The music; are you dancing?

The Dance

What's the name of the song playing in your life? How is it causing you to dance? When I think back over my life, it puts me in mind of a dance, where it seems the song never changed. Although the faces and places are ever changing but the way I reacted to them remained the same. Changing partners, moving around the dance floor, and even changing the way I move when dancing continued to leave me completely empty. I'm inspired and love all kinds of music. While writing this book I listened to music and found strength in it. I found myself changing the song ever now and again to give a new boost of inspiration.

Can you imagine your favorite song and how listening to it over, and over again inspires a positive feeling inside, but as time moves forward the hold on it weakened. The first thing that comes to mind when I fall in love with a song is, "I could never get used to hearing it", but in time, I do. The inspiration I found in it is no longer needed. Will I ever forget that song? No. I will always remember it and would love to hear it from time to time, but going on to the next best thing is a possibility I want to explore. The song is how you live life, but the dance is how you react to it.

Although, secretly I dance alone, I enjoy having a partner as I believe many do, wanting to share your dance with another is natural. The song is the influencing factor that helps you choose a partner. Different characteristics are brought out by different types of music.

Like a slow jam, hip-hop, or gospel music. All very different genres, creating different reactions in the way we dance. The song of life changes the way we dance, this is why I ask, what song is playing in your life, and how are you dancing? How are you living your life? Are you frustrated with the song on repeat unable to hit the next button?

Since I'm a lover of music I cannot imagine not being able to explore different kinds of music, being motivated by someone else's experiences, and learning I'm not alone in the dance of life. As I dance to the song playing in my life I notice, I'm not alone on the dance floor. I remember going out to a club to listen to music with others, and on the dance floor you see all kind of personalities. You see someone who dances with their eyes closed, someone completely out of control, someone who cannot dance with the beat of the song, and the person who's dancing alone. I noticed when in these places the dance floor is always a bit darker than the club.

Sometimes it would be so crowded you couldn't see who you were dancing with; Scary huh? Not so much, in that moment of dance, sometimes depending on how much you like the song you could dance with anyone. The music in the club would be so loud you couldn't even hear yourself thinking, you would almost have to give yourself over to the atmosphere you were in to be satisfied with the experience. Meaning if you were looking for a quiet place to meet someone new and carry on a conversation, going to the club is not the place.

Think about it, the club is a place for non-verbal communication, trying to get to know a new personality through talking will not happen there. Body language is the communicating factor, if you don't have it, you were unable to speak. Not everyone listening to music knows how to dance; they lack experiences. Music is about expression, and the dance is driven out through the passion of one's life. You dance differently to a song you're unable to relate to, but if you can relate to it, than your dance changes.

I believe every single person on this planet can dance. It depends on the song and being true to themselves when allowing the music and what it says inside to bring out the correct form of dance. Example; a ballerina dancing to hip-hop, can she attempt to relate the same form of dancing to hip-hop as she would classical music, yes, she could, but would it be appropriate? Why not just give in to what her dance is design to do. Staying true to yourself allows the world to enjoy the uniqueness of you; given yourself over to a false identity only leaves you accepting a false sense of who you are. In this frame of mind you will never be satisfied.

Life is a dance; can we enjoy life if the song being played is disliked? What if the song being played is not favored by your dance partner? How then will you dance? You probably won't be dancing at all. To be frozen in life unable to move forward due to the song you are not able to dance will age you quickly. While in this frozen state the devil steals your youth. When in our youth we are strong and full of possibilities, unfortunately youth and ignorance walks hand and hand. Unable to dance wisely to the songs in our life, we waste absurd amounts of energy and time. Without the proper teaching and mentoring needed in our youth we dance out of control, off beat, and with our eyes closed. We don't care what song is playing we just want to dance, we ignore our partners and dance with everyone, only when the music stops and the lights come on do we realize whom we have been sharing a dance.

Who picks a partner in the dark? We do, when dancing to the music being played by your life long enemy. Every song played by him attacks your vulnerabilities, and desires. He feeds the neediness in your life to keep you coming back for more, leaving you unsatisfied and desperate. Preying on our weaknesses are the traps he sets to ensnare us. Being trapped by the devil's music is easy, but an escape, not so easy. Should it happen to you, begin following the guidance of your inner man and not your mortality which is smothered in emotions and corrupted with defeated tactics. Let me explain, your inner man has the knowledge you need to escape.

The use of human knowledge will not be adequate; it does not have the right combination of power to withstand the attack of the enemy. The weapons used to destroy us are disguised, they are made to look natural, but they are supernatural. When thinking on how deadly it can be for us when ignoring the enemy, puts me in mind of the gun. Think a little on how it works and what really injures or kills, it's the bullets. The force and power behind the bullet is the gun itself, but not without someone to pull the trigger.

The devil knows how we work, in everything he does it's a format and a plan behind it. He wants to destroy us, but first he has to get us to dance to his song. We know some of the ways we could be killed because the human body is very fragile, but the devil knows how to destroy us from within. His number one priority is to keep your eyes closed while you dance. If we were to witness the ugliness of the devil you would not accept him. He's smart enough to know that the human race has a huge weakness, and that's to enjoy the ugliest parts of life completely based on how it feels, not what it looks like.

We base decisions and life changing choices on how it will make us feel, not on the end results that can ultimately kill us. Example; the drug addict, the alcoholic, all basing a decision to continue use on the fact that it feels good, and numbs a painful void, temporarily satisfying the unquenchable thirst to avoid reality. What song is causing your body to live a life without purpose, aging it, and destroying the assignment of the inner man? When the inner man becomes smothered under the abusive hand of the enemy it is unable to help you find your way off the dance floor. This poisonous, seductive song is being played to lure you into his trap reducing years of life, stealing your youth.

Do you know what song is being played in your life? How is it causing you to dance? The weakening of the body is part of the plan, as you age the body changes, growing tired faster, and even stricken with illness. Without the body the destiny within is unable to come into maturity, it never blossoms. Just as a seed, purposed to be a flower can never bloom if the proper amounts of sun and water are not received. When dancing to the devil music you are in no position to mature in the purpose God has for you. Like that flower, you are not receiving the right nourishment needed to provoke the gift within.

Ultimately in this Tween Place you are just passing time in a dance, to a song that is sucking the very life out of you, in this passage I'm referring to the life being sucked out as the very source of life itself the spirit man. When destiny cannot be activated in your life, your life force dies. Thinking back on my experiences, when going out, brings to mind how on entry to a club, you had to look the part. Whoever was the doorman had to made sure before you could enter you looked similar to the atmosphere of the club.

Example, if that club was into drug use, or other illicit acts, than you would have to dress the part to get in. Under the suspicious of the doorman, if you did not fit the profile, you were not allowed to enter. To dance in the Tween Place you must look the part, being able to fit in with the crowd. The bible tells us, about the broad road that so many will travel. The broad road possesses its own tune; and with each person a different dance. Most people respond differently to the devils music; however it continues to render the same results.

To be ensnared by the seductive tones of his songs is deadly. Overtime, by listening to his music, the works of evil began to demonstrate its power in your life, and you suffer greatly. The most troubling thing I've notice is when something is forbidden, in this state of seduction, we crave it more. During the course of the book I have been identifying different characteristics of the enemy plan, the different forms of attack. Now I will open your eyes to another tactics he uses when we dance to his music. Being separated from our Creator and not knowing our purpose in life, is one in the same. Without the Creator the purpose does not exist, we need to find Him first.

Who searches for someone they don't know is missing? There is a torture at play in our lives. My effort is to shine light on the stones of sin that has fallen into the great ocean of life; causing the ripples of consequence; which has led to depression, repression, and suppression. By helping you to identify these hidden traits will start an awakening of our true selves. When ignoring the voice within daily, tumbling down the rabbit hole becomes like breathing. Severe anxiety is born, amongst other little forms of mental sickness. Unfortunately not knowing where the bottom will be increases the chance of these breakdowns. I have not in all my acquaintances met anyone who did not enjoy music, or love to dance.

The songs of life should bring joy, inspirations, enlightenment; that will promote love. When choosing what songs one should listen to, it should be those that bring these special qualities mentioned above. That brings another point to mind; if you are attempting to do anything in life, think about it first; how will this decision cause me to dance. Nonverbal communication speaks loudly, but we as a people are so familiar with listening with our ears, we forget to pay attention to the silence. Being attentive to how someone moves takes love, it's a selfless act. Many do not possess it, because in today society selfishness reigns.

We are so busy with all the technology; texting, and emails, etc... We don't need to look in the face of the one's we love to know their okay. We just take their texts, or emails. Trouble can be spotted in the eyes of your child simply by the way they look at you, or the way they move; body language is a very loud silent communicator. The dance can sometimes identify the songs without even hearing it. Pay attention to those you love, but first before you can recognize the dance in others you must confront it in yourself. You will notice it in someone else if you are freed of its hold in your life.

Start to accept the truth that is being revealed to you, and watch for the positive demonstration of God's power in your life. Life is a battle, and since we are destine to fight, wouldn't you rather be on the winning team? God will equip you with the weapons of power to defeat the enemy in your life, but first you must say yes. That's right, prepare for battle!

The Battle

The Earth is no stranger to war. It has suffered many. Sometimes I'd picture the Earth as a human being and wonder; if it could talk, what could it reveal to us about lessons learned. How could it illuminate our minds to all its knowledge and know how. With all the tragedy of war, what is it all for? Why is the battle necessary? I'm thinking no one wants to go off to war, leaving the comforts of home, friends and family. Only to face an enemy who may or may not know your name, who doesn't care about your skin color, age, or gender; caring only about whose side you're on.

That's it. What we as women have failed to realize is, we are in the midst of a battle daily, and whether we are choosing to fight or not, makes no difference because you are automatically drafted in upon birth. You have already been enlisted. I will not even try to speak on war in a way of stating I can relate in anyway, because I cannot. I have not lost a loved one to war, or felt the effects of war to the point that I may say, I know what it is like.

My country on the other hand has experienced war, and has suffered great loss. My heart has felt the sorrow of knowing lives have been taken due to terror, and blood has been shed to protect me and my children. The men and women who fight to protect the United States of America, do it, and without even knowing the names of every citizen of whom they are protecting. I believe it is good enough for them to protect the people they do love and know well, without knowing everyone else. When looking out at our military, I see many soldiers with many individual reasons for being, and that makes up the purpose, they have made their choice.

One brave man per family to represent his or her small part of our great America, coming together to fight. I am amazed by it, and forever grateful to every single soldier that fights for the nation I live in daily. Thank you. Just as a country has to be on guard, in constant alert and attentiveness so must we. I can hear the voices of people in communities where I once lived, and remember the older women sitting on the porch of their houses speaking about how different things in life affect people.

One day there was a new program on television speaking on a murder of a woman and her kids, a jealous lover committed these horrible crimes. As they begin to watch comments begin to surface, it seemed everyone had an opinion. Some were like, wow; that's sad, and others, where a bit more negative, stating the girl should have known he was crazy; as if to blame her for her death and the death of her children. That amazed me, I was like…Wow! Stories of horrible things happening to good people seem to be the topic of our lives, but it is only when these bad things happen to us personally do they become life changing.

Yes we can hear bad news and feel empathy and yet forget about it in the same minute. It is not until disaster darkens our doorstep and then we feel pain. The battle that we experience in life should not be only viewed as a national crisis where war takes place, but should also be seen as a personal one. My point, when thinking of a battle on a grander scale it becomes dismissive because it's not in your backyard, so why even care? That's why I'm here to shine light on this hidden evil, and make you aware of the battle that's happening right now, not somewhere in a far off land, across miles of water, but inside of you; a battle that is not about gaining control over land, but gaining control over your soul. What better way to take you hostage then to keep you in ignorance that you are being hunted. Without acknowledging the battle we give ourselves over freely.

Just like if you were to ignore the fact that you can't swim, and jump into the lake; what could possibly become of that; drowning is a strong possibility. Not a fact, but a possibility, for all I know, in your panicky state of mind, you could save yourself, stranger things have happened. Why wait for the possibility of survival when there is a certainty of it through Jesus Christ. What I want to relay in this chapter is the fight that must go forth to ensure your survival. I will be helping you to realize the mandate of knowing which side you are on. I want to aid you in the choosing of living life or just choosing to continue to exist, only when a choice has been made can you truly begin to live. So let's now begin to focus on the personal battle within ourselves that ultimately leads to our fate.

I would like the focus of this chapter to make clear these very important points. Although, for me it can be very difficult to put into words everything. I will try to keep it simple. I will do my best. When thinking on the battles we face, three particular characteristics come to my mind. I want to touch on the experiences that I've been through to give more insight on how greatly crippling these particular characters affects you in the battle for your soul. The first I would like to touch on is "desire". I look at this word and I feel its meaning, as if it's burning a hole through my chest.

Let's take a close look at the definition of desire; to wish for, long for, to request, it could be a sexual urge. Desire is something I began to feel and experience as a girl. I desired so many things; I will try to focus on the ones that shape my personality. Desire has the power to control you, to rule over you, it can command of you whatever it wants. Desire is like a drug it's so very addictive, created to make you feel good, weightless, like floating into space surrounded by hope, and eternal bliss.

It is time to shine light on desires that are empty, destructive, and accompanied by pain that's so incredibly deep, almost never able to return from it. The effects of desire is seen throughout your life if you could just stop and rewind taking a good look at how many things in your mind are rooted in desire. How many of those things are actually at work in you now, and how many have come to life. I'm not talking about a wish, I'm speaking of desire; that driven urge powered by the fuel of a passionate pursue backed up with tons of emotions. When thinking on desire and its beginnings, I imagine soil in a field as far as the eye can see; it looks perfect for the planting of seeds.

The soil is moist, healthy in color, soft to the touch, just right for the sowing of a beautiful harvest, a farmer's dream field. I believe in the eyes of God when looking down on us, in the most beautiful time in our lives when we are children He see that beautiful field; being filled with hope, with all the right kinds of seeds awaiting a bountiful harvest, bursting with life. This being God's original plan for life, unfortunately as we spoke of before in the previous chapters, things have change, and so have we. The field that's ready for the farmer is one that has been weeded out, tilled, and plowed. In the same way we are to prepare ourselves for the planting of seeds, and made ready by the sacrifice His life ensured us, the wonderful harvest.

First, the battle must be fought and won. It's not enough to want to fight but you need to develop a mindset to win as well. God's Holy Word give us all we need to be successful in our efforts, all we need is to submit to Him and be willing to obey whatever He would have us to do. Getting to know Him is priceless. Without the studying of His Word it's useless, nothing will come of it but pain, and frustration. Trust me. I have been there living my life blindly at the mercy of people feelings, and messed up hearts. To become strong for battle, Christ and all that He is must be embraced.

You cannot simply be in transition you need to know beyond a shadow of a doubt that He comes first and He is number one. On the battlefield the devil will sift you out like wheat. The challenge for many women is dealing with tedious emotions. We do not possess the power to deal with our emotions alone. I have learned the hard way that my emotions have to go through Christ Jesus. He has to purify those uncontrollable feelings and teach me how to handle them. Desire is rooted in emotions; that's when it becomes so dangerous to have uncontrollable feelings.

Feelings that are rooted in someone other than God, when you place your heart in the hands of people you have set yourself up for such destruction that I'm unable to truly put in words the pain you are welcoming. Having a wild desire to please others or have their approval is a void that only God can fill. Being swayed by an influential person due to your desire to please or gain approval will always leave you empty and searching. With Christ Jesus that search is over, He will accept you for who you really are flaws and all.

He will help you see yourself clearly, and show you how to make that image you see a reality. Desire is like a spring roll filled with secrets. Secret urges, wants, aching for all those contaminated behaviors that render deadly results. The enemy is busy planning each and every detail of our destruction, one by one. Sin is smothered in secrets. Cravings I experienced at an early age were strong and confusing. Not quite sure why they even existed. I just remembering wanting to do the very things that had the power to destroy me, not knowing at that time it was even possible to crave sin that way.

My body was feeling all type of things and my little mind was conjuring up all types of evil. Television aided me on in my fantasies, whatever I saw on TV I begin to crave. My body reacted to certain scene in a movie that involved a love scene whether it was passionate kissing or a bit more, I begin to feel desire and I liked it. My little mind started to search for the movie scene in real life. I wanted to make it come true. Desire began in my mind, and my body longed for what it had seen. This is why I can stress the important of being cautious as to what you watch on TV as well as what you are allowing your kids to watch. Trust me, it matters. The Bible tells us the eyes are the light to the spirit, what are you allowing to enter you through your eyes? The Bible also explains that we are born into sin, and until we accept Christ as our Lord and Savior we continue to live and grow in that sin. Think about it, everyday outside of Christ we become more contaminated with evil desires, therefore killing our soul.

There are so many blessings in this life God wants us to experience, changing for the enhancement of your life is worth it, not just to save your soul but also to reap the blessings He has for you right now. To walk through this life without His forgiveness, mercy and compassion is to live in fear, regret, and depression. You may be saying "it's okay",

I'll take whatever life throws at me with no complaints, but I refuse to allow the enemy to win the battle for my soul. He creates all types of destruction for me on this planet, and then I turn around and give him my soul too? Join me, and put an end to the secrecy, let's expose the plan of the enemy together.

Expose the hidden desire, shine the light of Christ on those empty cravings, and destroy the enemy in the light of Christ. Nothing can escape the light. I hear a lot of women confess they want to change, but never put their wants into action, you won't change anything in this life just simply wanting to change. A deeper search must be implemented into your life for results to be seen. I had got to a point where I was exhausted with false start, and declarations. Trying to master my desire only took me deeper. You cannot master desire it must be uprooted with the Word of God.

There is no other way. Test what I am revealing to you with the Word of God, and see that it works. You cannot say you have changed if God didn't cause that change. Only God can uproot behaviors like desire, and empty cravings, we cannot simply meditate these things away. They must be removed like a cancer that kills the body. Just think, cancer only destroys the body, but sin destroys both the body and soul. It's not like we have to wait until the dangers and tragedy of sin manifest or until we die, we can witness its sharp knife as we live every day.

The Bible tells us, the wages of sin is death, and you better believe, you will get paid. Think of all the different personalities we take on due to secrecy. Secrecy is as cold as the grave. It only holds what is dark, and unfruitful. It's selfish, deceitful, and vicious. Secrets have been known to destroy families, friendships, and nations. Hiding in the dark places of your heart are secrets, the very things you need to expose to be set free; are hidden within. Secrets cause you to alienate yourself from love and the people who can help you. You tie the hands of friends who really care when you keep secrets, no one can really know what to do if you are not up front and honest about what is hurting you.

To get on the path to recover is simply admitting there is a problem, a secret, a struggle. You must confess that you are a sinner first in order to be forgiven by Christ. Acknowledging that the problem exists is the first step. Sometimes it's unclear the struggle, the problem, and the secret. You may not realize your issue, so how can you confront it? Uncovering the depths of a behavioral problem isn't as easy as it sound. This is because secrets are buried so deep inside the mind, until eventually it's like a decaying tooth it can't be ignored. The pain of that secret becomes a sore spot in your life, if anyone even reminds you of the pain you break into millions of pieces. Rage, angry, and resentment floats to the surface of your heart leaving you wondering all the while what you are feeling. I know it has happened to me a couple of times, in my past relationship; getting mad at the new for the pains of the old, and never really recovering from past hurt just moving along but not dealing.

When you keep secrets you are not dealing you're avoiding. Avoidance is not the answer it will eventually run straight into denial, then resistance, never really embracing the truth. The truth in this case would be whatever reality you are in not necessarily living. With so much denial in your life you live in a fog like haze, never seeing yourself clearly. When you are unable to see yourself clearly you become whatever people say you are. Are you beginning to see the dangers in secrecy? It all has an ending, these untamed desires and cravings in life all send you traveling in circles, until you reached your end, based on your tolerance.

I'm just thinking on how Jesus was letting us know in the Word of God that He did not come to Earth to bring peace but a sword. (Matthew 10:34-36) That means, He came to divide and separate the worldly relationship of mother, daughter, father, and son; to unite us in the eternal bond of sister and brother through His blood sacrifice on the cross. The bond of spirituality is stronger, and greater than that in the blood that binds mother to child. The gifts of God are forever, the gifts of this world is temporary and will perish. So why invest your heart and soul in something or someone who does not share an eternal bond with you. When thinking on the destruction of secrets I find myself searching within to seek out what is hidden in me.

I want to expose the very things inside me that cause me to be the way I am and shine light on anything that is affecting me in a negative way. Secrets can separate you from God; they can cause a struggle where it's not needed. I found that when I pray God begins to uncover the hidden places inside me that I'm not dealing with, disappointments, hurts, angry, etc… When you accept Christ into your heart He makes everything so very tender, on the inside you feel like you're melting as if your heart has been frozen for years. As your heart melts, the tears are endless.

Those tears become your prayers; they speak for you as you wail. Some hidden area are revealed and tears are all that's left, no words can be found to describe the hurts it's just too deep. That's fine because He's listening it's no one else's concern, just between you and God, He's listening, so go ahead and cry it is okay. Secrets are like inner demons controlling your emotions they have power. Inner demons have the power to tell you how to feel, who to trust, and never to commit. Their controlling everything, your very decision making is under the power of this spirit, born of your secrets.

These inner demons love their home inside of you and feed daily on the negativity being produced because they exist inside of you. Inner demons grow stronger as time progress because the secret grows more powerful the longer their withheld. The secret creates a nesting place for spirits to control your life. When growing up I had dreams of what I wanted to be and do, but making bad choices detour all those dreams and I became my consequence of sin, and that was not a good me. As a matter of fact, I became more tangled in the web of deception caused by these controlling spirits as they whispered I listened, keeping my secrets and burying them in a casket lowered six feet deep, I buried my pain.

I felt the voice of God always calling for me to turn to Him when I was hurt, but I always turn in the opposite direction. Why did I do that? No sure, I don't think I wanted to believe in the good. I prefer to run after the difficult, the bad. That in itself is a spirit, when you run from the very peace of God to dance to the destructive music of the devil you know controlling spirits are holding you captive. That's right you are a prisoner being held captive by controlling spirits that are using your body to sin and eventually taking your spirit to be placed in eternal fire; where they will celebrate their accomplishment forever. Don't give yourself up so easily, begin to embrace the truth in this book and know that this Earth is meant to fight the battle of life to establish eternal life with Christ Jesus.

Stop building your kingdom here but rather prepare your soul for Christ. Help me and others spread the message of the Tween Place to free the hearts and minds of those being held captive. When embracing Christ you are agreeing to tell the world what He has done for you. It's my responsibility to shine light on everything you are reading right now, and once you have read this book and have decided to embrace its truth you too must share and shine light in the dark places of the world. Remember your world is no bigger than the community around you; your brother, sister, mother, father, and friends. Keep it simple, you don't have to travel across the country to relay the message of Christ, start with your neighborhood. Who gives you the boldness to battle the outer defense of the devil? The Christ within you gives you all the power and boldness you need, when you embrace Him completely trust me, you will not be able to shut up. Don't be like me and drag your feet, move in the present and for once in your life put the devil on his guard.

You will be ready for whatever he thinks he can throw at you upon finishing this book, open your ears and hear what the spirit is saying to you. A lot of situation I knew to walk away from I walked into anyways causing me to learn the hard way, and some were not so much my fault but nevertheless I still had to learn some powerful lessons. Those lessons were to stop blaming others for the things that happened to me. When stuck in the blame game you get nowhere it's a trick to keep you in the land of resentment. Next you'll find yourself making excuses for why you can't succeed in life because of whomever you're blaming.

Once you enter the land of resentment the next drop off point is in the place where no one forgives, and now hatred grows in your heart and it goes on and on. You see sin only progresses; you can never say what you wouldn't do when you're in sin because its only grows. Like weeds in the field sin will consume you and take you over if you don't surrender your will to Christ. He came to bring life to us and to create in us a new heart, capable of love and compassion. More importantly I had to learn not only does He place in you all that's good, but He places inside of you Himself. By doing this you learn that it is not you that has to face the tactics of the enemy but it is Him. He stands from within, and shines so bright that the forces of evil cannot even see you. You become more than a conqueror through and in Christ Jesus, but first you have to decide to allow Him to live within you.

Another battle faced within is the burden of past memories, hurtful ones, they are like negative seeds planted by an over seer of your childhood, a significant other, childhood bullies, family members, or a religious mentor. No matter who did it, it was done and it hurts. That took a lot of time to admit, to admit I was hurt, disappointed, and carried it in my heart for years. That's right, facing the pain, admitting you are broken in parts of your heart the very core of your existing takes Christ. No one can lead you to that well of confession and expect you to drink freely; it takes the grace of God to face the pain.

When you have experienced the hurtful things done to you by others after a while who did it to you become irrelevant, but the pain, "my God" the pain, is very relevant. You can try to forget who hurt you, but you cannot erase the pain, that pain that follow you everywhere, no matter where you go, or do, pain follows. The thing about pain is it produces an addiction, you will find yourself searching for more of it when the burden of the previous ones become a distance memory. I would awake some days in so much pain, I would be like, where in the world is that coming from, I couldn't remember the "why" or "who anymore just the pain. So, that told me no matter if I chose to remember exactly who hurt me didn't matter as much anymore.

The fact remained that the pain doesn't go away with time as people has sometimes predicted, it just does not disappear, you have to go to battle with it, it must be dealt with, not erased. You cannot erase the scars within, you need an internal healer. Time does not heal wounds inflicted by loved ones, or anyone who mattered. Even the people who didn't matter, "matters" because the power of the tongue is deadlier than a double edge sword, the cuts travel very deep, and natural remedies cannot heal them, you need Christ. I tried so many different paths to seek out healing and they all lead me back to Him.

Going down those paths left me so empty and I returned after reaching a dead end, more messed up than I originally started. As, they say I walk in, but returned limping. You have to surrender that stuff inside that's fueling the raging pain. That raging fire is how you are living your life sowing hatred and reaping negative results. The very meaning of your existence is smothered in a daily routine of repetitions causing us to feel like life is just a big endless circle of control. We become engrossed in the chase to live life, which we actually don't get to live at all. What is living? Living is discovering the awesome gift of Christ healing and being made whole.

You may be thinking I am old now I have lived the best life I felt I could live, is it too late for me? The answer is no, it is not too late for you. The minute you decide to give yourself over to Christ life will begin for you. His timing is not our timing, He will redeem time, and life in Him will begin. Being of an older age and no longer in your youth, means nothing when Christ is involved, and also being older doesn't take away the wounds life has inflicted on your heart, as a matter of fact the need is that much greater for you. You need to get that pain up and out of you, and be filled with forgiveness; forgiveness of yourself and others. Christ enters in and cleans house. He will heal your heart and mind; He will do much more than that.

Eyes have not seen, nor have ears heard the things that Christ has in store for you. Let Him in, and be healed! When thinking on the chains that held me to my inner prison my eyes fill with many tears, and my stomach feels like it has 75lbs weights in it, so much pain. Only in Christ will the questions your heart is longing to be answered will be given to you. Only in Christ will you understand the big question we all carry in our hearts "What's this life for?" You want to know the answer? Get in Christ, your answer is in Him. Stop asking all the right questions to all the wrong people, ask Him. Remember the chapter on pathways, asking questions to all the wrong people will lead you down so many wrong paths only to reach more confusion and to become more dismayed, go to the Source, seek Him out, He will answer. He will answer with the clarity you need so you are able to see yourself clearer.

Do you know your true self? Do you know your place in the battle? Who's side are you on? The real you is the part of you that is ignored when choosing not to embrace the Creator of life, and the gift His Son gave to the world. To ignore Christ and His sacrifice you are ignoring the real you. Getting to know the real you is embracing the Son of God, when you embrace Him, you are embracing your true self. Everything you are is in Him. Everything you are meant and purposed to do is in the embracing of the Son, there is no other way. A lot of people focus on Heaven as their ultimate goal when accepting Christ as their Lord and Savior, but I have come to realize, Heaven in its entire splendor is not the focus of the day, but the focus is in obedience, submission, and my destiny.

I have to fulfill my purpose in the Earth, and not just to sit around waiting for Heaven. When Christ removes the blinder from your eyes and allows you to see yourself a chain reactions kick off. I call it going through the motions, because that's what happens, your emotions flood in like a severe thunder storm. You can feel and see all the signs that a storm is brewing and headed your way, take cover. The sensitivity that happens after Christ touches you; it's like coming to life after being numb or frozen. You will begin to feel everything that has been locked away inside of you for many years and will continue to feel everything as you go forward, but the difference this time is you are not "alone" you are with Him and He is with you.

Another part of the battle within is the inner fears we face. Fear is so dangerous and paralyzing causing a pause to everything flowing forward in your life, including your existence. What's makes this so dangerous is time doesn't stop and will not freeze. When frozen you can't react, move, live, or do anything worth doing. You know, the things in life that really matter, your eternal self alerts you to what must be accomplished, your purpose. Even the very things you do outside of destiny, has a purpose. Everything has a reason for being, why should you feel that you don't have a reason for existing. Don't think ignoring or living your life in fear takes you out the battle. Ignoring your place in this war will not save you from the end result. It is better to come out of fear and face the reality of your purpose and take your place on the battle field, than to hide waiting until it's over. Signs that fear are a struggle for you are when committing to anything that is difficult for you, causes you to run, even when it's something as beautiful as Christ Jesus.

Fear and its crippling effects will weigh heavy on your heart. It doesn't matter how nice the offer is when fear is present commitment goes out the window. Not being able to get pass the "what if's" of a situation always plagues your choices. When I struggled to commit to anything including committing to committing, I was terrified at all the things that could go wrong. Being in fear caused me to always focus on the negativity it was like second nature. I became a great target for the enemy; he would use my fear to cause co-dependencies with people; stuck in confusion, inventing a false life to cope.

He used the voids in my life to make me needy and dependent on others. Example, I was caught in the trap of not knowing the difference in loyalty and people pleasing. Being misled to think, when being mistreated sticking around was loyalty. I was being emotionally beat down and at the same time paralyzed with the spirit of fear, fear of the unknown, fear of change, and the fear of rejection. My God, I was tied up in some serious chains. Everything inside of me was screaming to escape, the path of escape was shown to me, not only could I see it, I felt it, but fear caused me to second guess my escape. Fear caused disbelief, I didn't trust my intuition, I didn't trust the voice within, or myself.

Staying in situations where you are being abused will cause all kinds of side effects. You suffer great emotional damage that takes the grace of God to repair the damage. Think of all the resentment you are breeding. The effect on your self-esteem, are detrimental. The one thing I remember most is the useless feeling of being at the mercy of other peoples mood swings, and selfish tendencies. What a horrible place that was to be, trap inside myself, holding the very key to release myself, scared to venture out into the unknown. Think on it for a moment, is it better to stay in a cage of fear in the dark, than it is to open it, step out into the dark to seek out the light in your escape? When living your life in fear you never really trust anyone, but you will sometimes trust your own effort to arrive at some type of decision, in doing something.

You become lost when relying on your own strength. Fear gives birth to decisions based on all the incorrect sources of information. Decisions made out of desperation will not make it far, because fear eventually subsides. We have a way of running from the things that scare us, or completely suppressing them altogether. Fear, the list is endless of the strongholds, and effects it has on our lives. Unfortunately, the way we find ourselves after being lost in a fear making decision is washed up and injured. Thank God, not dead. I believe that even in the struggle to come out of fear, we learn powerful lessons like; knowing how to transition when things in life change, being more adaptable. In fear, change is forbidden. You can do a lot of things to a person whose life is governed by fear, but change is not one of them. Remember in Christ Jesus no spirit has power over you, not even the spirit of fear. Always remembering God has not given you the spirit of fear, but of peace, love, and a sound mind.

Fear has so many faces, those faces can come in the form of a trusting love one, with all their negative thinking and fears; stay away from people like that, until you are able to stand in the boldness of Christ and face your frenemies. Learn the power in blocking the negative no matter what form it enters. When you are able to get past fear it will not matter who it is, you can stand, and go to battle. Learn how to say "no" and stick to it. Set a standard of acceptable behaviors and influences in your life; don't allow the devil to walk all over you.

Embrace the boldness of Christ and stop running, "fight". I would rather stand, fight, and die; than to run in fear and be killed anyway hiding. Put on the amour of God because it is the only protecting force of life we have for the battle ahead. The shield, and sword, is the inner weapons of Christ put into place to aid in the defeat of our enemy. The battle within must take place before the outer battle will be won. Gain control over your life with the weapons of power given to us in the surrendering all including the spirit of fear to Christ Jesus. Once the surrendering has begun, then the rebirthing can take place. Have you reached your due date? Do you know what it means to be born again?

THE REBIRTH

You must be born again, said Jesus to Nicodemus. Nicodemus was a member of the Jewish ruling council, he came to Jesus one night and said, Rabbi we know you are a teacher who has come from God. For no one could perform the miraculous signs you are doing if God were not with Him. Jesus replied, "I tell you the truth, no one can see the kingdom of God unless he is born again". Nicodemus asked, "How can a man be born when he is old"? Surely he cannot enter a second time into his mother's womb to be born! Jesus answered, "I tell you the truth, no one can enter the kingdom of God unless he is born of water and the Spirit. Flesh gives birth to flesh, but the Spirit gives birth to the spirit. You should not be surprised at my saying". You must be born again.

Again Nicodemus asked, "How can this be"? Just as Nicodemus was puzzled at the words that Jesus was speaking we also struggle to understand the plan of God. Jesus was speaking of a spiritual birth, an awakening. In the world, we are governed by what we see, touch, or feel. We struggle to believe the unseen. Believing in what we cannot see is the very act of faith itself. Can we embrace what Jesus said then and know it still exist the same today? Yes, because the power of His words are still very active and real, we only have to decide to believe.

> For God so loved the world that He gave His only begotten Son that whosoever believes in Him shall not perish but have everlasting life.
>
> (John 3:16)

Jesus goes on to say, that God did not send Him to condemn the world, but to save the world through Him. Whoever believes in Him is not condemned, but whosoever does not believe stands condemned already because he has not believed in the name of God's one and only Son.

> Jesus continues to say, this is the verdict: Light has come into the world but men loved darkness instead of light because their deeds were evil. Everyone who does evil hates the light, and will not come into the light for fear that his deeds will be exposed. But whoever lives by the truth comes into the light, so that it may be seen plainly that what he has done has been done through God.

Being born again is a spiritual act of cleansing the soul with the truth of God Holy Word. Although you don't actually go into a physical womb to be reborn, in faith you enter the spiritual womb of God. The cleansing power of God washes over you from within, outwardly the evidence can be seen. It becomes visible in your life, behavior, and the way you think; it is noticeable in your walk, and talk. Nothing about the light of Christ shining from within is hidden from the world. Christ tells us to let the light shine, so that men can witness Him on the inside. Christ wants to be seen, if He is within you He is not a secret. I remember years ago when God was revealing the transformation we feel when accepting Christ into our hearts; the transformation feels like a shock to your system, your body and its current stance changes. Thinking on my experiences; I remember feeling a bit conflicted. My mind had thoughts of its own; my body had desires that were not in line with this new choice. I attempted to control my moods, and desires with just willpower.

Failing continually, I felt as if I could will those behaviors away. I began to struggle with keeping God's wishes. I found myself making mistake, after mistake, after mistake. Then I would confess out loud, "this is too hard", I'm not able to do this. I was trying to master salvation through my own might, strength, and will. This was a misunderstanding of the choice I just made to serve Christ. Thinking sin could be mastered, I had a lot to learn. Being a newborn in Christ Jesus is just that, you are new, and have quite a bit of growing to do. Be patient with yourself. It is a must to be born again; there is no way around it. I must stress the importance of understanding that being a good person without being reborn is in vain.

Living life as a nice person will not get you entry into Heaven. The only way into Heaven is through the Son of God, you must be born again. Christ Jesus was sent to Earth to create the way into Heaven, and only through Him will you enter, there is no other way. Through the rebirthing process you will feel and see the active power of Christ in your life. Don't you know we serve an active God? He works. Ask Him to forgive you of your sins, invite him into your heart, and welcome Him to clean and make you ready to start again, with Him. This is the first step in being born again, it starts with confession. As I listen to the news on television and opinions here and there, I've hear so many thoughts on what people say God wants. His Word explains His wants and requirements, just His Word, not peoples opinion. In sending His Son some believe Jesus to have come for a certain nations of people, but through it all He came for the world. Being reborn allows you to confront life without the guilt of your past. Christ has forgiven you, and remembers it no more. This is His Word. You are free to start anew with a sense of awareness, and conviction. Both are needed to keep the purity of your choice.

We cannot do it alone, this is the reason He rose from the dead and ascended to Heaven, then leaving behind the Comforter. In doing this He knew we needed assistance, guidance, as to how to build on our new foundation of life. In the book of Acts, chapter 1 verses 9 thru 11, states the promise of Jesus that he would not leave nor forsake us that he would always be with us to the end of time. He fulfilled this promise in the form of the Holy Spirit sometimes called the Comforter. The Holy Spirit dwells within the believer and will dwell within you. (Also see Matt 28:20, John 14:18) We will get into more detail about the Comforter and who He is to us in the upcoming chapters.

Go ahead and read those scriptures and familiarize yourself with Him and the purpose He serves in your life. (Ephesians 5:8-10), tells us how to walk in love, to walk in light, and wisdom; all very important baby steps to take as a born again Christian. Keep your eyes on the prize. Stay focus on Him, with all your heart and mind. Know the importance of spiritual guidance at this point. Listen to the leaders or elders of your church. Express any struggle you have with integrity. The new light of your decision helps to keep things out of the darkness. You will want to expose the things that keep you tangled up. In the book of Ephesians, Paul goes on to explain the importance of pulling off the old, and putting on the new.

Again, this cannot be done on your own, you need the Holy Spirit. Prayer, communication with God, hearing the Word of God, and studying His Word, are all keys to walking out your life in Him. (See Ephesians 6:10), I love the book of Ephesians, because it keep me on track reminding me of the new position I have in Christ, I am alive, I have awoken from a deep dying sleep. I must fight to stay that way. The scripture reminds you, to be strong in your new birth; you must learn to stand for what you now believe, that passive attitude must go. Stand firm. In this stage you must understand the answers are not your answers, it will take a moment to acknowledge that your knowledge and interpretations of things are not going to help you in your new birth.

You must become like a child eager to listen, therefore you will learn. Being coachable is not a natural ability, especially in those who don't like being told what to do. I have heard many times when I'm speaking to my children, and ask them; "what did Mommy just say?" you should see their faces; totally blank. They were not listening.

Listening is a skill. Being coachable comes from being humble and having a yielding presence. Allow yourself even when uncomfortable to submit. You have to become uncomfortable to reach the place of comfort that awaits you. You have to get past yourself to get what you need. I remember my baby moments in Christ, I was ready to scream to the world everything God had done, although testimony is good, never go alone to face all those you have turned away from; instead be with a brother or sister in Christ that is mature to back you up. Trust me the enemy is waiting to trample on your innocence, and take advantage of you. Example: if you were an alcoholic would you return to the bar after months of not drinking? Don't rush to grow up, be in God's timing and you will survive.

When being reborn you have a heighten sensitivity. Everything begins to feel tender. Be patient with yourself and those around you. Try not to feel like people are telling you what to do all the time, or they are simply trying to control you; this is a trick of the enemy to try and get you to run away. Don't fall for it. When accepting Christ as my Savior, there came a level of accountability. I had to be accountable to someone, and at that time it was my pastor, or mother who was also in God. Who answered my questions and pushed me to read the Word of God. These individual also kept me in prayer, giving me solutions when problems would arise. They helped me, stay clean by keeping in sight my choice and helping me to honor my choice.

By pointing me in the right directions and giving me spiritual knowledge it was their job. It is important for you to have that mentor to give an account of your day. This will help you. Don't just get saved and run away from the church, because guess who is waiting? That's right "sin" and all his friends. Don't get caught up. When growing up my mother was always trying to keep us out of her mistakes in life. She would always say, been there, done that, it's not worth it. Trying with all her might to help her girls avoid some of those pitfalls. Did we listen? No. You will have to make the decision to listen to people who have been placed in your life to guide you spiritually and avoid the pitfalls that Satan has waiting for you. The devil's trick is to make you feel like you're giving up so much.

Well, you are giving up a certainty of death; remember that when he is trying to torment your mind with the past. The struggle of becoming new is in trying to hold on to the familiars, by not accepting the path that lies ahead. This is the stumbling block for many. We have all been down that path before, listen to your guide, the inner man, and lean on your leaders for support; as they should always direct you to Christ, He is the only answer, all roads lead to Him. Just go ahead and accept that you are in the learning curve, and it is time you buckle down and follow the leader. Can you see the outlet?

The Outlet

Congratulations! You have accepted Christ Jesus as your Lord and Savior, you are born again. You have chosen to let Him be your guide through and out of the Tween Place. In this chapter I will be revealing the passage out of the Tween Place. Living in this world but not destine to reap the harvest of its destruction. The outlet and place of freedom was sent to us and confirmed through God's Holy Word.

In the book of John chapter 3 versus 16, he tells us; that He so love the world (Tween Place) that He gave His only begotten Son that whomsoever believes in Him shall not perish, but shall have eternal life. In that scripture; I learned at a very early age the power of God's divine plan to create a departure for all who will believe. His Word confirms that His Son Jesus Christ is that outlet from a perishing world. When you believe in God's plan for our escape, you must understand why the escape is necessary in the first place. Many have heard the message of Christ and have been touched by it, and in the same action unable to go forward in the new life Christ has brought to them.

This is the effect from a lack of knowledge, and comprehension of the choice. When hearing the message of Christ being delivered by the pastor, or friend your heart opens to the possibilities of His love, you want to know more. Especially when hurting. Once you decide to take that leap of faith, a new world opens up to you. In my experience,

I became aware of the behaviors, habits, and conversations that were not pleasing to Him. It was like a feeling in the pit of my stomach, or an inner voice that whispered "don't do that", "don't say that".

My experience receiving Christ was an active one, He was real. When receiving Christ I didn't necessarily look at Him as the way out of a convicted world, I didn't see the bigger picture. I didn't understand the power that had just entered my life. I had been changed forever, and didn't really know it. I began to grow up, making tons of mistakes, and being told by the older Christians what not to do all the time, it just seemed like a job I never signed up for. It felt hard, confusing, and just too much work, I thought for a young person. I don't think they realized how much that sucked the joy out of my life, and made me feel I was not ready for the choice made.

That was definitely not what God wanted for me to feel. He wanted me to feel the joy of my salvation, the peace that comes with the decision to choose Christ. I'm not saying you have to know everything to live in Christ but you need to understand what being in Him really means. This knowledge doesn't happen overnight, it comes with time, and experience. Some, you will read about in His Word, and will not understand until you are ready. Being ready comes with studying and giving different parts of your life to Him in an act of surrender. That takes me back to helping you understand your way out, the outlet.

Tell me, who searches for an exit when they are not ready to leave? Who tries to escape when they don't know they are in jail? The key in accepting the Savior is to realize you needed to be saved. This book helps you to understand where you are, and the need for an escape. We are not alone in our attempts to finding the oasis in the desert of the Tween Place, Christ is with us. We need only accept His help and allow Him to lead the way. In the chapter that discussed the reality check, it brought us into the knowledge of what's really going on, and how we must confront it.

Now we have awoken to the seriousness of the past, and we now must accept responsibility for our actions, ask forgiveness, and welcome the outlet into our hearts. It is time to come away from the excuses, and the casting of blame. We must stop living life through our pain; it's time to step into the light of Christ. When rejecting responsibility we cannot become free, we can only embrace the possibility of freedom and continue to dream. Christ is not a dream, He is a reality. The way out is a journey of confession, deliverances, and a pulling off of the old and a putting on of the new.

When accepting Christ as your Lord and Savior, you have elected to take the journey, which leads to everlasting life. I have heard that life's a journey, but who wants to meet the end without the key that opens the gates of Heaven. To journey without Christ Jesus is to journey in vain. The journey begins with a choice, and what lie ahead is the passages out. As you begin to walk, know that you are stepping out into the truth. The truth of who you were, and who you will become, and what that means.

Now that you have chosen Christ He will lead you. Just picture a forest filled with many paths as I discussed in a previous chapter, and only one path leads to eternal life. When following Christ it caused me to take deeper looks inside my soul. On this journey when following Him, He leads the way and as you travel through the passage He teaches you His Word, which brings clarity to the confusion of life. In that clarity He helps you to release all the conflicting memories that keep you weighed down, and unable to travel with Him swiftly. Stepping into the truth cannot be received without stepping into the decision to follow Christ first.

Now that we have acknowledge the first step let's begin our journey through and out of the Tween Place. Making the choice to take the passage out is a spiritual one as well as physical, but remember it all start within. To exit one's life and enter into another is the start of seeing yourself in a new light. Putting into motion a chain reaction of surrender forms the mileage and brings you that much closer to your destination. Let's deal with the act of surrender. Surrendering all things that hold you back, that are in your grasp.

Surrender is keeping you in motion and plays a great part in helping you keep up. The kingdom of God is preparing itself for the arrival of God's people, it is in motion. Meaning we need to stay in motion, and how that comes about is in the surrendering of all hindrances you know you have with prayer that exposes those you cannot see. As you journey He is preparing you for entry, take nothing for granted. Stay focus on what Christ is revealing to you, don't take what He has given to you and put it off on another. His words for you are for you.

In this journey and at this time it's between you and Christ, become stronger in your faith, then one day you can stand firmly to strengthen another. You will know how. Coming out and stepping into the truth can sometimes make you feel mortally sick, because of your emotions. That's why the strengthening of your spirit is the key and Jesus will guide you through how to sustain as the truth washing over you. The experiences you are about to encounter is all for the good, you are being refined like gold. Yes, you will feel the heat but at the same time you will not be burned; the peace of forward movement after being frozen will satisfy your troubled mind. The evidence that Christ is working in you, will be the proof. You will see, you will understand, and with understanding you can forgive, love, and live.

So many times outside of Christ I have felt stuck and lifeless, but even when I had to confront everything in life that hurt me and to relive those moment of truth, I have never felt more alive. Once I remembered and accepted what happened and began to deal with it, confront it with Christ Jesus, no longer did I have to rewind it like a movie in my mind. He healed me and took the pain away, so when that memory would rise again, it had no power over me. Understand that life has some terrible memories, the kind that make you want to drink them away, but in Christ Jesus, that urge to drink and drown that pain will no longer exist. He is the fountain of eternal life.

You can drink of Him and never thirst again, so go ahead, stay in motion, and when those memories, that painful memory creeps up into your mind, drink of Him, and thirst no more. During the journey you will learn to surrender all, when the load becomes light and you keep traveling with all confidence in your guide. You are becoming stronger in your faith and the clear reality of the Tween

Place clearer than ever. You no longer hold on to it, it has become a distance thought, and memory. More importantly you have realized you don't need it. You began to accept your boundaries, and in that acceptance you have learned to lean and depend on God.

As you follow Him you trust that you can surrender all those past hurts, everything now exposed, by the light of His presence, given to Him. You began to understand how He takes even the bad and turns it and uses it for your good. You have accomplished a lot by getting past what you were feeling to seeing the choice you made was good. Taking responsibility for mistakes made as you journey and confessing the need for help. Needing help, you finally turn to Him. You are growing. You feel that inner strength don't you?

As you journey you begin to see how powerless you were in the Tween Place without Him. You're learning as He reveals the mysteries of the world, and a wave of fear causes you to tremble at the thought of life without Him. Coming into Christ cannot be a decision made out of fear; you must decide to follow Him because of His sacrifice, Him loving you first, Him being the gateway of life, and being the very essence of our existence, reunited. When I speak of fear, being afraid of Hell is not enough, that reason alone will not keep you in Christ. It needs to come from love. Allow the drive to live to become the force that motivates you beyond your fears, with time it is possible to convince yourself not to be afraid. You can dive right back into bad habits of creating false realities to cope. Stay focus. Remember your motives and keep them pure. Pure motives keep your mind right and you heart clean. In this way fear doesn't stand a chance.

The motive for choosing Christ was one governed by a need to end your oppressions, to be freed of the cost of sin, and your love for Him. It takes more than a temporary fear of Hell to make this journey and finish. You must want it for real, more than life. The pull, or what I like to call "the tug" of Christ calling you to go deeper, study more, pray harder, is what grows inside of you as you grow closer to Him. When following Him you should be feeling the need to equip yourself with the weapons of power and make ready your body, and spirit with the armor of God. As we come up out of the Tween Place on the path of righteousness we will encounter the tricks and trades of the enemy. You will need to know how to fight; can you say, training day.

Training Day

In the book of (John 20:24-30), Christ was revealing himself to the disciples after He rose from the dead. He was able to show Himself to eleven of the twelve, and then again with them all present. James was not present at the first revealing, Jesus came again, to appear to Thomas and show him that He had indeed risen, and to rid him of his unbelief. In doing this Thomas was able to see, touch, and prove Christ truly had risen. In verse 29, Jesus told Thomas; because you have seen you believed, blessed are those who have not seen and yet believed. Christ appeared to His disciples to also leave with them a gift.

He knew in His absence they would need power, courage and comfort for the path ahead. When repenting of your sins in the name of Jesus Christ, you will be given the gift of the Holy Spirit to empower the change. When Christ ascended to Heaven, He knew we would need a guiding power, an active weapon against the devil. Christ knew the devil would form great attacks against us. He did not leave us alone; He left behind Ultimate Power, the Holy Spirit.

> In (John 16: 5-15), Jesus tells us the purpose of the Holy Spirit. But now I go away to Him who sent me; and none of you asks me, "Where are you going?" But because I have said these things to you, sorrow has filled your heart. Nevertheless I tell you the truth. It

is to your advantage that I go away; for if I do not go away, the Helper will not come to you; but if I depart, I will send Him to you. And when He has come, He will convict the world of sin, and of righteousness, because I go to my Father and you see me no more; of judgment, because the ruler of this world is judged. I still have many things to say to you, but you cannot bear them now. However, when He, the Spirit of truth, has come, He will guide you into all truth; for He will not speak on His own authority, but whatever He hears He will speak; and He will tell you things to come. He will glorify me, for He will take of what is mine, and declare it to you. All things that the Father has are mine. Therefore I said that "He will take of mine and declare it to you.

You are blessed! Understanding the power you have ushered into your life through Christ Jesus is important. At this stage you will need to learn how to activate the power of the Holy Spirit in your life. I would like to make something clear; the power of the Holy Spirit and His presence in your life is a gift, He was given to us. There is no way of earning Him, He was not given to us based on anything we have done, and He is a gift. When given a gift, what do you say? Thank you Jesus, and show Him your gratitude by the demonstration of obedience in your life.

Believe in what you cannot see, trust Him, be blessed. In all honesty, I have seen more in not seeing than in seeing. The power in believing is the secret in seeing. If, you are experiencing doubt, know that you are not alone. There is power in reading the Word of God. It will help in the tearing down of unbelief that is rooted inside of you. Training is all about believing, understanding, establishing your confidence to use the weapons of power in Christ Jesus. Preparing for the daily battle is essential; however the spiritual one is equally important. As, a twelve year old girl, I wrestled with the spirit of unbelief, always second guessing, and reasoning with the things of

God. Then one day I felt a presence, the Holy Spirit. He spoke, and said, "You have a spirit of unbelief". He guided me to the Word of God, and when praying I would be delivered.

I believe Him, and begin to pray, and read my Bible out loud and yes, that spirit left me. I was able to believe without question in the name of Jesus. It is very important for you, in this point of the book to understand that, knowledge without believing is powerless. You must recap, and think, do I believe? It's time to become empowered with the power of the Holy Spirit, struggling with your belief can no longer accommodate you on this journey. Leave it behind, step now into your faith, and receive your power.

I've dreamt of fighting with evil spirits, knowing the words to fight, and yet on the inside I was fearful of what I was encountering. That fear was paralyzing and hindered the active power I was given through Christ Jesus. I had to realize that believing is more than knowing the right words. Believing is action, bold actions to stand before all and confess Christ is Lord, no matter the cost. The power in activating the manifestation of His power is in believing. I can show you the way in many detailed analysis, but you must walk out your destiny. Again the power is in believing, you must believe. He has forgiven you, believe it. He has given you the gift of the Holy Spirit, believe it. One night when I was a young girl, I awoke with the most terrible headache; actually I had been suffering with it for three days or so. I couldn't take it anymore. I found my mom who was up late reading her Bible. I was crying and tired wanting something to be done, anything. At that point I was fed up, and desperate. I was willing to try anything, including the most dreadful of medicines, I just wanted it gone. So, I approached my mom and explain my pain, and how long I had suffered. She looked at me, and went on to say, "here read Luke 10:19", handing me the Bible. I said ok, but at the same time thinking, just hand me a pill. I went on to read,

> Behold I give unto you power to tread over serpent and scorpions and over all the power of the enemy and nothing shall by any means hurt you.

I finished, and look at her and said "my head stills hurts" she said, "keep reading until it goes away", "don't just read it; believe it". What do I have to lose? I began to realize God had given me power over the forces of evil.

> Ephesians 6:12 tells us, for we do not wrestle against flesh and blood, but against the principalities, against powers, against the rulers of the darkness of this age, against spiritual hosts of wickedness in Heavenly places.

God has given us a detailed description of a very real enemy, in that moment I knew who was the cause of my pain, sickness is not what God wants for the body, and it's not His will for us to be in pain. I began to read the scripture, over, and over again, until I believed in the power of what I was reading. Not even six times when the pain in my head completely went away. It was gone! God healed me, with just the reading of His Holy Word. I shook my head and looked at my mom and said "wow" it's gone. I went to bed praising God, from that night on He began to be more than a church going experience, he surpassed what I heard, He revealed Himself to me as God, and whatever I asked for in His name, He gave.

That's why understanding that believing is the activating element is priceless. Are you ready to receive? In this chapter I will be opening your mind up to the power of God through His Son Jesus Christ. There is so much training that needs to be administered that you will need to also be attentive in church, listening and receiving each time what the Spirit is revealing; equipping you with the weapons of power. In the book of Acts, the Disciples of Christ received the Holy Spirit; they were filled and began to speak in tongues.

Also, Paul crossed paths with the disciples of John the Baptist and He gave them the message of Christ and they believed, and were also filled with the Holy Spirit, and spoke in tongues. Being filled with the Holy Spirit gives the boldness needed to face the world with the message of Christ. You need the power of the Holy Spirit. You are no longer lead by your ideas, but by the spirit. (Romans 8:9-11), tell us;

> But you are no longer in the flesh if anyone does not have the Spirit of Christ, he is not His. And if Christ is in you, the body is dead because of sin, but the Spirit of Him who raised Christ from the dead dwells in you, He who raised Christ from the dead will also give life to your mortal bodies through His Spirit who dwells in you.

You have now through Christ Jesus become alive; The Father gave the Son, The Son leaves the Holy Spirit, what an incredible plan. Learning the importance of the Holy Spirit is needed in maintaining your salvation, and reaching your assignment in Christ. Living life "double minded" or as Paul puts it in the book of Acts 8, "the carnal mind", is to live in a defeated state; this state of mind will not submit to God. In Verse 8 of chapter 8, stresses the importance of being in this way of thinking hinders your relationship with Christ. The Holy Spirit gives life to our bodies, and illuminates our sight to see the Spirit and recognize the assignment. Becoming spiritual minded is needed in overcoming the cost of sin in your life, and experiencing the power of God.

Recognizing the spirit and its goodness and in vice versus recognizing how sin is killing the body, mind, and soul. Through Christ resurrecting power we are given a second chance, and with the power of the Holy Spirit we won't waste it. Don't continue to live one more day outside of God's gift to the world, His Son Jesus. Receive and believe Christ's gift to you, the Holy Spirit and all He brings into your new found freedom. Acknowledging the enemy, we can equip ourselves accordingly. I identified him earlier, now let's learn more. He is a threat not to be taken lightly; he is real and ready to destroy you the first moment he gets a chance, by any means necessary. You must prepare. He has been given many names; the devil, Satan, the father of lies. In Matthew 4:1-11, he even tried to tempt Jesus in the wilderness during His fast of forty days and nights. Every time he spoke, he failed. Jesus didn't argue with him or throws stones; He simply used the Word of God. The devil will come, and bring along with him those cunning words of influence; how then will you drive him away, if the Word of God does not exist within you? The Bible tells us in the book of (Peter 5:8-10),

> To be sober, be vigilant, because your adversary the devil walks about like a roaring lion, seeking whom he may devour. Resist him, steadfast in the faith, knowing that the same sufferings are experienced by your brotherhood in the world. But may the God of all grace, who called us to His eternal glory by Christ Jesus, after you have suffered a while, perfect, establish, strengthen, and settle you.

Simply screaming at the devil will not move him; you need the Word of God, the name of Jesus, and the Holy Spirit; to be equipped with the boldness to face the enemy. The devil is the father of lies; he is not capable of telling the truth or does he understand it. In the book of (John, chapter 8:37-47), Jesus was explaining the difference in Himself and those claiming to be the descendants of Abraham. He was identifying the difference in who they claim to be versus who they were really.

How many say, I am saved because I go to church every time the doors open, but are not living their life in Christ based upon God's laws? That type of behavior will be exposed, just as Christ exposed them. If you're not living in Christ, don't claim it? Those people whom Christ was speaking, accused Him of all kinds of wickedness, but He held His ground calmly and spoke the truth. You don't have to argue with people who speak against you, let your life be the evidence in your case. Let the Spirit testify of your character. Walk the walk and talk the talk.

You are proven innocent by the fruit you bear. People can be very harsh, disrespectful, and will just flat out lie. How do you deal with these types of problems? You don't, Christ has justified you, you have no need to explain or justify yourself. Remember, accusers may even be close loved ones, a special friend, or even your spouse, the list goes on and on, but who should the battle always be with? How do you forgive and move forward? Do you think Christ had room to carry around in His heart the list of accusers, and betrayers? No, he kept His heart pure, He had a job to do, and He knew who to battle.

We must also follow in His footsteps, failing to believe this powerful truth is the defeat in every battle you face. People only have power over you, when you fail to forgive. Failing to identify the devil at work in your life through the people you know or don't know will lead to pure misery and a defeated life. How many times have I heard people complaining that God is not answering their prayer? He has answered your prayer when He sent His Son to be the example. Everything you need answered is in Him. Not only is Jesus the answer in overcoming these obstacles, He identify the real enemy. In identifying the devil, He revealed the power in how we can avoid becoming offended by others. We don't have to walk around holding grudges. We can forgive. The devil is the real enemy, and through the Holy Spirit we can defeat him, and his group of minions. Get mad at the devil, fight the devil, and make war with him when he is attacking your life and the lives of those you love. Get the training you need to face your adversary. Equip yourself with the weapons of power. Remember it starts with believing. When accepting Jesus you became part of His body, (1 Corinthians 12:13) explains how the body of Christ has many members and all those parts are made of us, each one given a unique purpose.

Although we are different we are united in His body. That's why confusion in the church makes no sense; Christ body has no foundation for confusion and it should not exist. All members of His body are placed in the care of the Holy Spirit; all are baptized in the spirit. We must maintain unity in the body of Christ, the Spirit does not simply hovers, He dwells within. Training consists of learning not only to have divine wisdom, but to live wisely; not to just know of faith, but to walk by faith. As you grow in Christ, active qualities should be noticeable, teaching others of God, serving others in love, to give" not grudgingly, or out of necessity, but cheerful giving. Compassion should shine from you. When Christ enters in everyone will know, He is not a secret, so don't attempt to make Him one. Training also consists of becoming strong, in the book of Ephesians Paul explain how being made strong is only in Christ, we cannot do it ourselves. Stop trying; it will not be by might nor by power, but by the Spirit that we succeed. David in the book of (Psalms 27) put it so well when describing who is the light of our salvation.

> The Lord is my light and my salvation whom shall I fear, the Lord is the strength of my life of whom shall I be afraid. When the wicked came against me, to eat up my flesh, they stumble and fail. Though an army may encamp against me, my heart will not fear. Though war may rise against me, in this I will be confident.

David knew where his strength dwell, his power, and boldness all in the Lord. That same confidence has to dwell in us as well. By using the wisdom and examples of those before us we are always able to push forward. Be empowered, and know that you're not alone. Stop living in a defeated mind frame, rise above it all. (Ephesians chapter 5, verse 17) tells us,

> Not to be unwise but understand what the will of the Lord is, and do not be drunk with wine, in which is dissipation, but be filled with the Spirit.

> Come away from confusion, lets us do as Paul instructed the church, speaking to one another in psalms and hymns and spiritual songs, singing and making melody in your heart to the Lord, giving thanks always for all things to God the Father in the

name of our Lord Jesus Christ, submitting to one another in the fear of God.

Being trained to handle the battle in life is necessary, but let's not ignore the battle with ourselves to line up with the Word of God. Knowing your life is in God's will is not just words of completion, but in the manifestation of the Spirit in your life. Prepare for battle, it's time to get dressed. In the book of Ephesians, Paul describes getting prepared for battle like a suit of armor; the breastplate of righteous, as a person character, and deeds; Girded with the truth, your integrity, a life of honesty. Your feet shod with the preparation of the gospel, the gospel being the very foundation we stand; your shield to be used against the devil fiery darts and all types of wickedness. The devil cannot penetrate the shield of faith; your helmet of salvation, and the sword of the Spirit. Knowing the Word of God, the specific Word to use in any given situation by studying intimately can be achieved?

God's Holy Word is the weapon of power, but what good is it to you if you simply hold it in your hands for décor and never read or study? You may scared those who just look at you, but those who attack will win, due to you not knowing how to will the power of your weapon. What's the use of pretending, especially when pretending is so hard, and eventually it will come to a horrible end. Get empowered for real, before the devil calls your bluff. Separate yourself from all distractions, during training you have no room for corrupt company. Evil company corrupts good habits. Stay focus. Second Corinthians chapter 4:2 tell us, how the world struggled to understand Paul's way of teaching, and made accusations, be careful in trying to convince others who are so set on defending their way of life that they try and twist your words. In these situations, use the spirit of discernment, and be led by the Spirit. Always remember you don't need to convince people of the truth, all you need is to continue speaking it. When you find your words being rejected, simply walk away. The battle is not yours, it's the Lord's; Meaning, always remembering with whom we fight.

Learning to keep your cool is through a daily workout in prayer. In prayer, you find your connection to Christ. Staying in constant communication with Him will built and inspire your daily walk. In John 17, Jesus showed how he was in constant communication with His Father. He prayed for His disciples, that they be protected from the evil one. He made it clear that they were no longer of this world, and were living according to the Word of God. He prayed for their sanctification of truth. He prayed for the Believers, you and me. There is power in prayer. It strengthens you, like refueling your car when on empty.

In the Garden Jesus prayed in His approaching the fulfillment of His purpose, to carry the sins of the world, and became separated from His Father. He was sorrowful, and distressed, but His destiny was bigger than Him and He had to push pass and through with prayer. He asked His disciple to watch and pray that they don't fall into temptation, because the spirit is willing, however the flesh is weak. Training to understand the purpose of prayer is in knowing how you cannot trust your flesh. Prayer keeps you in the will of God and moving forward. Don't ever think for one second you are completely under control, because in that thinking alone, the flesh is at work. Never underestimate the flesh. Keep it under the power of God. We all have a cross to bear, and the weight of that cross may seem unbearable, but through prayer you will see, it can be done in Christ Jesus, nothing is unbearable. Only through prayer can this be realized, you must learn to pray through. Jesus teaches us the power in what we say when praying.

We must always pray for God's will. Adopting perseverance and patience in prayer are essential. We must pray for His will in everything we pray for, His will. Sometimes the weight of what you're carrying seem heavy, don't pray it away; instead pray His will be done, regardless. Always His will. We have to learn to stop praying away our troubles, stop avoiding our problem; we must face them and go through in the name of Jesus. Prayer will see you through to the other side. Pray through. Sometimes we look for all the fancy words to talk to God, He doesn't need all that, pray from your heart; and when you can't find the words, always pray that His will be done, no matter how you feel.

Continue to say "Heavenly Father your will be done, Holy Spirit take control". You cannot go wrong when His will is being done, regardless of what it looks like, or feel like. It's His will. Trust Him. When going through and fighting with the enemy, praying is like kicking it into survivor mode; you have to want the will of God more than breathing. Everything in the name of Jesus, only in the Name of Jesus will you get the attention of the Father. Recognize the power of the Son. The world is forgetting with all the positive thinking, and meditation, they are forgetting the cross and its purpose. Let's not forget the Son; everything through the Son. In (Matthew 28:19-20), Jesus came and spoke to them, saying,

> All authority has been given to me in Heaven and on Earth. Go therefore and make disciples of all nations, baptizing them in the name of the Father and of the Son, and of the Holy Spirit.
>
> Teaching them to observe all things that I have commanded you, and know, I am with you always, even to the end of the age.

There must not be any doubt found in you; Christ is the Son of God, be ready to scream it to the entire world no matter what, non-negotiable. Struggling with the belief of Christ at this point in the battle is very dangerous, that's why it is of the upmost importance to saturate yourself with the Word of God, and keep lifted up in prayer anything in your life, not lining up with the Word of God. If you sense you are in trouble, go get help, your sisters, brothers, or pastor in Christ will aid in praying you through. God sees your need before you even say it, He will direct you. Where we lack, He fills. (John 4:24) tells us,

> God is a spirit and in those who worship Him must worship in spirit and truth.

How can we worship God if we are not in the truth, or in the spirit? Knowing what it's takes to live this life in line with God, is in the studying of His Holy Word. How can you know Him if you never read? How can you talk to Him if you never pray? How can you know who is the spirit of truth if we never seek it out? How can we seek it out if we never become aware that something is missing? Join in the battle to help awake a sleeping world to the knowledge of who's missing. Can you imagine how very scary it would be to reach the end in total ignorance? Or would it be worst to reach the end with the knowledge and not have shared it with anyone? What will it be like for the person who heard but did not listen? Who seen but did not believe? The manifestations of God are all around us, we are a manifestation of His power; the proof is in the mirror.

In (Philippians 4:6), Paul tells the Philippians,

> Be anxious for nothing, but in everything by prayer and supplication, with thanksgiving let your request be made known to God, and the peace of God which surpasses all understanding, will guard your hearts and minds through Christ Jesus.

Trust Him, he will show up. I've learned in my walk with Christ, when fasting accompanied by prayer, and studying the Word a clearer connection to Christ was reached. I didn't encounter the struggle in my mind when seeking out His plan. I became more humble, more committed to His plan. Fasting is a necessity. You need to include fasting in your life, going without eating for whatever amount of time the Spirit is leading you, be obedient. You will know when to include fasting and how. Sometimes my will is louder than the purpose inside me, I needed to fast to make quiet that voice so that I would become yielded to the purpose of God. Fasting causes those stubborn parts of me that challenges the will of God for my life to line up with the bigger picture, and not just the present moment. If you are struggling within with a presence of evil in other words any behaviors setting themselves against God's will for your life, kill it with fasting. Push away that plate, get in your Word, and don't play with it, because it's not playing with you. Jesus was telling His disciples about fasting and praying in Matthew 17:21, they were asking Him about a boy who had a demon. They couldn't cast the demon out of him, and when Jesus did, they wonder why they couldn't, and He answered,

> Because of your unbelief, for assuredly, I say to you, if you have faith as a mustard seed, you will say to this mountain, Move from here to there, and it will move; and nothing will be impossible for you. However, this kind does not go out except by prayer and fasting.

When I think on this scripture, I want to utilize all that Christ has empowered us with through faith to enhance the kingdom of Heaven, starting with myself, getting in line all things with the Word of God. I cannot stress it enough, the importance of getting yourself in line with the Word, and then you can go out to harvest the field of God. It starts with you. A lot of people don't like the idea of giving up their meals to fast, but think of it as a bonus to get that much closer to Christ, and through Christ the Father. No one gets to the Father without the Son. Pray for wisdom, pray to empty out offenses (see Mark 11:25), pray to be delivered of the off springs of sin (see Philippians 1:19). Pray without ceasing, in everything learn to pray. In prayer you recognize your purpose. When contemplating for what is missing in your life, prayer reveals direction. When the answer comes to you, know that prayer was the key ingredient. In the beginning, God had a purpose for the world and now has a purpose for you (Ephesians 1:11), you may not have been able to remember that plan for your life because it was taken from you, but now through Christ Jesus you have the power to wage war on the devil. So, go ahead, take it back.

Taking Back Destiny

Sound the alarm, you've been robbed! Once you have acknowledged the need to sound the alarm you can form a strategic plan to start the search with an action plan, not a thinking plan. Many times we fantasize of who we want to be, but never doing anything. Fantasizing keeps you in a cycle of wasteful thinking. It doesn't direct you into the harsh reality of it never falling on your lap, or being left on your doorstep. The greatest battle in taking back destiny, is tackling that lazy way of thinking; which inevitably becomes a way of living. You have to get off the couch and seek it out.

Laziness is the defeating presence that we as believers cannot afford to have operating in our lives. Using that saying "I'm waiting on the Lord", stop with the excuses. God is ready for you and has always been ready; you can't say you're waiting for Him, when He is waiting for you. Stop fixing it up, and get moving. When you are seeking Him, His Word tells us He will not hide from you, when you knock He will answer. The harsh reality; there are no excuses. Satan has stolen from you, and guess what? He doesn't think you even care, because you won't get off that couch!

You have been robbed! Even the person who smells the rain carries an umbrella. It's time to stop talking about it, and be about it. It's time to get busy. Wishing on a fallen star will not get you there. Positive thinking will take you in cycles; only in Christ Jesus will you succeed in anything. Come away, this day from the excuses. I wrote a blog name "The Blame Game" it goes over how we use people who has hurt us as reasons to stay in a defeated life. The truth is we are why we are in a defeated life when we can't accept what Christ has done. Christ has freed us from the oppressions of our past, and placing our feet in the place of liberty and success. A destiny that seemed thrown away, He took back from the devil when He went to Hell and took the keys of life and death. He has all power, and through Him we have the power to take back our rightful place.

Laziness is crippling and causes us to think that purpose does not exist, or that we are too old, whatever the reason, stop justifying it with excuses. As for the why's, who's, and that are keeping you from purpose, let's focus on that person in the mirror, holding you back. I found that in my efforts to get off the couch, I failed over, and over again. I had to accept my failures, and release that anxiety over to God. I began to ask Christ for His forgiveness for my laziness, with prayer. I had to trust Him to deliver me from a hindering spirit. I asked in His name, and He did it. The more I read, the more I came to terms with His plan for my life. I begin to want what He wanted for me, in this world seeing my place in the great design.

From personal experience I know the struggle of setting off to take what has been stolen. When I came into the knowledge that I'm more than what the world see's me as, I craved it more than anything. Destiny began to grow within, and screamed for an out. What's that screaming inside you? Satan's goal is to convince you that destiny is complicated, but in reality, all that you have done outside of destiny is hard. Now through faith in Jesus Christ everything you do matters. Your destiny is simple, Christ is simple, He is not complicated. He is not so sophisticated that only educated people can access Him. Again. If, the message of Christ is coming across complicated to you, seek help, and ask that they make it simple. Christ is simple. His ways are easy and can be accomplished with and through Him, you see; He doesn't work over you or beside you, He works from within you.

In that alone you can see the power in conquering the devil. In this moment I'm thinking on love, and how very powerful love is; I've heard so many times how when love steps in logic and reason steps out. Love is unconditional, and doesn't keep score. God is love. He invented the definition when He gave His Son to die for the world. All the information in the world cannot teach you to love; only in Christ can you truly love. When you love, you stop rationalizing your destiny. Your relationship with Christ and destiny is tied together. To love the Lord is to obey Him. Obedience is how we show Him our dedication, our love. Sitting on your couch claiming you love Him, and not seeking out destiny is not love. You are in disobedience. When you accepted Christ as Lord, you also in the same breath accepted destiny.

You cannot have one without the other, we don't get to sort through God's Word and chose what to live and what to ignore. We must conform to it all. We are not to take from God's Word, or add to it. It is what it is, take it all, or leave it all. We have to face in this generation how the Word is solid and we are to change, not the Word. God is the same today, as He was yesterday. He does not change. The manifestations of His power are operating in the lives of those who understand this. No one should have to identify that you are only quoting scriptures and the power of God is not in your life. In prayer you will see for yourself how you most govern your life with the whole book, not just certain scriptures. Alone time in prayer is essential to this becoming a reality. Prayer brings clarity when accompany with studying the Word. Prayer aids in keeping the mission of taking destiny back in your sight constantly.

It's like writing it all over the walls and ceilings of every room in your house. How then, could you ignore it? I at one time wrote on my bathroom mirror what I needed to accomplish in Christ Jesus. I needed to pray more, I needed to read more, and in Jesus name I wrote.. Every day I looked at the writing in the mirror and I began to do it, even if it was short, I prayed. When reading I read only a chapter, but I read. Eventually I began to do it on my own, without the writing in the mirror. I changed the writing to something else I struggled with until that was gone. With every request I wrote, in Jesus name. Always in Jesus name, never without Christ; never. Prayer kept me exposed to the sensitivity of the spirit, and helps my destiny become more than just an interesting thought. It helped me accept the manifestation of God's power in my life. It strengthens me to want it, without the fear. That monster of fear is a defeated foe, through Christ Jesus. God's Word tells us, He had not given us the spirit of fear, but of love, peace, and of a sound mind. Fear is not of God, which means you don't have to be entangled in the bondage of fear. Be in Christ, and come out of fear. I speak that in your life right now, In the name of Jesus. Fear cannot, and will not consume God's plan for your life. There are no flaws in the design God has for your life. I've heard some that may say, I am not sure what I am to do, please know, your destiny is not a guessing game. There is a solid answer for you; destiny has been design for you just as sure as the lungs are designed for breathing. Forgive me, let me be clear, God does not make mistakes.

Destiny cries from within us, especially when it's being ignored. It's like a newborn, you cannot ignore the cry for long, and not without consequence. and not without great consequence. I cannot stress the importance of staying prayerful as you take back your destiny. I know we have reasons to believe we are not ready or don't believe all together. There exists a great need inside of us to actively pursue destiny, and that need is getting pass yourself to focus on the task at hand. Destiny. No matter how you say it, and the many ways you strive to convince those who hold you accountable, that you can't or you won't, remember you cannot fool God. Give it up, in the end all that matters is you, Him, and judgment. None of the other people in your life who you are playing the blame game with will matter, so why should they now. God's Word gets you pass your emotions this is why it is vital that you read it. His Word is our very life force. Without it, we are dead. To live your life outside of your purpose is to live a defeated life, and to me that is death. Oh, how I suffered when running from the very thing that completed me, God's purpose, my destiny.

Hearing people when saying, "they are unable to get passed the hurts, and offensive acts committed against them". I agreed. Their absolutely right, they can't, but God can. He will change you, and train you in the weapons of battle to defeat the devil and his minions to take back your destiny. I can feel when a presence of evil is around me trying to sway my emotions, causing me to feel a sense of defeat. The devil is a lie; I wage war against him and in the name of Jesus, by wielding my weapons of power through God's Holy Word. The devil has no power or right in your life, he has been put out and must stay out, nonnegotiable. The bible tells us that it's not by might, nor by power, but by the Spirit that all things happen. What this tells us is that no matter how strong we think we are, we are not strong enough, nor by any authority we carry in the Earth, but only by the Spirit of God are all things possible.

The world wants God as long as it can dictate how it wants Him, but we don't have a dictation in the matter, God is God and answers to no one. His Word says we must believe in the Son, and only through the Son can we reach Him. There is no other way. Be careful of your sidekicks, cheering squad, and surroundings. All can be a key ingredient in the recipe the devil has brewing for your destruction. You may not be in the knowing right now as far as destiny is concerned, but guess what? The devil knows who you are, and has no intentions of letting you get away by discovering destiny. He doesn't think of you alone, he thinks of all that will be blessed and saved by the message you will release. He strives to keep you in the dark by all means necessary. That includes assigning demons in your life. The spirit of discernment makes you aware of your surroundings both near and far in the spirit. So, it doesn't matter if it's your friend or hometown, with discernment you can ready yourself no matter where the devil strikes. When you get your emotions out of the way, allowing God to lead, you will not care who is allowing the devil to use them. All you will be concerned with is casting him out.

When you begin taking back destiny Christ becomes your mother, father, sister, brother, and friend. He becomes everything. You need to lean and depend on Him. Tell Him your deepest, darkest secrets. Only allow in your life those He tells you is right, everyone else put on pause. Why is this so important? It may sound a bit cruel, but again, get out of your emotions, and get into the spirit. You have to in this moment trust God and His plan for your life. He is getting you ready to face a world you once lived amongst to take back what the devil has stolen. You can't help folks until you have helped yourself first. That's why I used the term "pause" you will pick up where you left off, but not as you were, but as you have become "empowered".

Those who cannot understand or digest the weight of your destiny must be stepped away from, to avoid unnecessary battles. You have enough to deal with in yourself without the outside interfences of those who cannot see the purpose on your life. No one has your purpose in their hands, stop looking to people to fill you up. They don't have what it takes, only God has your purpose and know how to get you there. Everyone has their shortcomings. People barely have time for themselves let along time for others. Basically, how long do you feel you can lean on the closest friend, or family member? Everyone has their limits for whatever reasons, but in Christ there are no limits, He is limitless, and welcomes you and all your baggage. There is no greater friend. Be aware of your surroundings, what you are listening to, watching on television, everything you do matters as you seek out destiny. Understand the vulnerabilities of your situations and taking nothing for granted, remain vigilant, and be mindful of the things you say. There is life and death in the power of your tongue. You could either encourage yourself or dam yourself with what you say.

If the person you hangout with is always coming with negativity, remember your condition and separate yourself until you are able to be there and yet be set aside. You can't be a part of something that can swallow you whole because you can't resist it. That's the purpose of finding your true self that you may know your identity, and not be caught up in someone else's opinions and beliefs. Your purpose causes you to be set aside, like a sheep, sent out amongst the wolves knowing beyond a shadow of a doubt who's your Shepard. You will need to step away from all emotional crutches, and trust God. It will seem like every single distraction invented is coming after you. This is a positive sign that you are moving in the right direction. Continue to saturate yourself in God's Word asking questions and addressing any concerns to your pastor or spiritual family for things you don't understand. The Word will provide you with courage, and strength to endure your journey. Be honest with yourself always. God knows you.

You cannot keep anything from Him so why try. Confess the things that become struggles for you, and watch Him work. Be sincere He is there for you. In allowing Him into your chaos, you are walking into His peace. That's the beauty of God, when His Son enters He brings with Him a light that shines in every corner of your being, leaving nothing in the dark. He sees it all, and yet He loves. In my quest to take back destiny I had to learn to shut out the negativity on the outside, but then when I got in a quiet corner the negativity in my mind was loud and powerful. I had to find a way to shut it off. Only through reading the bible and praying did this come about. Sometimes I would not pray, I tried to will it away. That did not work. Let me say this again, positive thinking outside of Christ is just a form of brain washing, and the effect of the process is temporary. I needed lifelong results, I needed Christ. Just as I convinced myself of one way thinking in that same way, as the wind would blow, I blew right with it. I was all over the place. My positive thinking was based in emotion. Emotion is like an ocean tossing all over the place, up then down. My God, I get sea sick just thinking on it. I needed a solid foundation to build upon; I found that in Christ Jesus. You can too.

Only in Christ can positive thinking exist, only in the name of Jesus. The mind and all its complication can only be transformed through the reading of God's Word; nothing else has an impact on it. It's a force within itself to be reckoned with. In the journey to take back what's yours encourage yourself, be your own cheerleader knowing you will arrive at your destination shortly. The Holy Spirit is with you, leading and guiding you through the forest of life He will never mislead you. The only real opponent is not even Satan it's you. Stay focus you can be your own worst enemy, stay humble; open to the criticisms of the Holy Spirit. Remember God chastises those He loves.

Don't ever settle for what life has handed you. You don't have to in Christ all things are made new, you have a second chance, go for it. Stop accepting the false win; you can succeed for real in Christ. Your purpose is still out there, you can still take it back no matter your circumstance, or age. Make the decision today to take back your destiny, stop settling due to fear, and disbelief.

Start by coming to terms with where your fear is rooted. Understand your purpose has already been decided, God doesn't need you to reinvent yourself. Wanting to be something other than who you are purposed to be is an act of avoidance. In your efforts not to hurt the people in your life, by surrendering to your call because they disagree is causing you to neglect, and see God's grand design. Just think of all the people you are meant to save through the message of Christ. You must come to terms with your destiny. Whatever your reason, don't be afraid to want it. You will find a peace that surpasses all understanding when you release the fear. Remember your destiny is bigger than you. You're not the only one in danger if it is never reached. In my experience of taken back my destiny I realized how bad I wanted to reach it, like a mother wanting to hold her unborn child. I had to confront my fear of wanting it, and thinking it would never happen for me. I was wrong to think that way. God wanted me to have purpose, and sent me into this world with it in tote. He has given destiny to us, and all we need is the courage to stand and embrace His plan for our lives.

Embracing Destiny

Look how far you've come! At this stage, embracing your destiny should be feeling like a celebration. My prayer is that you have received and believe what the Spirit is revealing through this book. While seeking out God's purpose for my life I read many books, but only when I read the Word of God did I find deliverance. All the different books and break downs of the message of Christ we're helpful, but should always lead you to God's Holy Word never away from it. I encourage you with all that you read, please spend most of your time reading the Bible, it's the purity of all others.

Keep your beliefs and focus in God's Word always, and remember praying without ceasing. Staying in communication with God is a vital life force, you will find life extremely difficult without talking with God, keep your knees bent before the throne of grace. You will need those very things mentioned above as you embrace your destiny. The Word of God keeps you humble; it repels reasoning and logic to help you grow in faith. The Word of God shows you the heart of God; you have to get to know Him in order to embrace who you are in Him.

Never think for once the enemy is not ready to come and snatch back what he once possessed. He is always trying, but when you are in Christ his attempts always fail. The characteristics of humbleness are mandatory in the next phase. Embracing destiny is embracing your purpose. In order to embrace your purpose you need to embrace the heart of a servant. I went through some challenging experiences that caused me to seek Christ in ways I never knew. These experiences caused me to search deep within myself to find the motive behind my choices. Those choices made me take a closer look at what was my driving force. What is it in life that moves you? My journey to embrace the heart of a servant was not an easy one. I will not lead you on by suggesting it will be easy for you, there will be some tough spots. Learning the lesson of servant hood can be summed up in a few words "becoming selfless".

In my heart, I've always wanted to help others. Always wanting to love on everyone, be kind, and having a continual smile. I love to bring a good feeling to any room. I smile, because deep down inside, I've always known God loves me. Seriously, I don't think I have ever felt like he did not love me. I have experienced heartache because of that open heart, and many disappointments. I have always had that "I think everyone is cool attitude". Again, and again with that attitude of always giving people the benefit of the doubt, repeatedly experiencing betrayals, one after the other. It was never in me to prejudge a person on any given level; I just did not feel comfortable. In my mind I would always think how I wanted to be treated, and then acted accordingly. I knew the basic law of sowing and reaping, and took it to heart, and there it remained.

As I began to mature in Christ I realized although I was trying to be nice I was not prepared to handle the rejection. My kindness was being rejected, my good intentions, rejected, my smile, rejected. It was if I hit the lottery for thousands of dollars in rejection. It did not take me years to notice people hurting my feelings; I felted it as a girl, teenager, and young adult. It was evident to me that this was going to be a part of life. I was the type of person who always wanted to give everything a reason an explanation. I had to know the reason in order to justify my acceptance of someone hurting me, and if I didn't have a reason the pain just lingered. That caused me to create one if one was not in sight, all I knew was I needed to cope; from a girl to adulthood what a journey of reasoning.

God's Word has always been here for us, but it seems to be the last place we look to for guidance. What a shame, because I think on how long it took me to simply embrace my healing, and how sick I had become with all the cancer of sin growing inside me. If you have not realized it by now let me enlighten you, God's Holy Word is no mere book, it is God's power harness between a cover. It's alive. There is nothing like it, read it, study it, and watch it transform your life. We in this world are willing to try some of everything, especially in the United States of America, but struggle continually to embrace the power that lies in the Word of God. Join me, and many others who are unleashing the power of God's Word. His power has always been at work in my life and the lives of my family. I needed Him so much as I began to notice how my life was not in a place of fulfillment; I was in a place of incompletion, sensing an incredible urge to do something, not really knowing what. Sometimes I find myself searching for words to describe the incompletion, but I could not find them. Such a huge emptiness, that brought on tons of negative feelings. With every bad occurrence that entered my life, the emptiness grew stronger, the agony that much greater. It affected everything, most of the time I simply wanted to just lock myself away and come out when forced. I did not make that transition outwardly, but I did inwardly. At least there I thought it was a secret. I wanted something so badly in life and it took me so long to admit to what that was exactly. I never felt like I had it, or even knew how to get it. I always felt like the odd girl, trying to catch up or fit in. I thought my silence was strength.

    Whenever I did open up, I felt my every word was being critiqued and no one really wanted to know what I actually thought, therefore not really wanting to get to know me. I began to become whoever I needed to be to get through or be a part of a relationship. I was embracing all types of personalities, becoming more and more like someone I could never recognize; further away from destiny. Thank you God for the life changing power of your Word; every negative situation I encounter whether I brought it on myself or not, I would find myself turning to God. When people hurt my feelings, I would feel Him there first. Most occasions I would allow Him to comfort me, and as soon as I felt better, I would either go back to the drama or find new drama. In those days I felt like I used Him to take away my pain whenever it became too much for me, which was most of the time.

I believe God sees the journey of all, and knows eventually life will lead us straight into His arms of safety. Those experiences came and went, but the scars remained, I never allowed God to heal me. I would go back into the world with low visibility to the plan the devil had set for me. Each and every time closer to my own destruction, it was the power of God that created an outlet in every situation I arose from, and have become able to speak of today. God's grace, His mercy that He gives freely as we trample all over His gift time and time again; but yet He loves. In my recklessness, He was teaching me a lesson. He was teaching me forgiveness, patience, and love. He was showing me how to forgive, because He forgave me. He was showing me how to love, by loving me as I constantly ignored His will. He taught me patience, as I discovered His way was the best choice for my life.

I learned the power of making His qualities a part of my life, even though I had not activated them until I accepted His Son, Christ Jesus. Christ endured tons of abuse, He set the example of how although He was God's Son, ultimately He was sent to serve. He was a servant to His purpose, just as we are servants to our purpose. The book of (John 13) tells the account of Christ purpose to serve, as He washed the feet of His disciples. In my learning of the meaning in this particular story meant, Christ was washing the disciples feet in an act of demonstrating the forgiveness of sin, but when I think on it I also see the humbling of service to destiny. When you take on the servant's heart you embrace the lowest level of service to become the highest level. It has happened many times in life were we see the rich man with the servant who takes care of his needs diligently, thinking only of pleasing his employer. He studies his ways, his likes and dislikes, his comings and goings. These lessons for the servant are not learned easily but they come in time, many years maybe. Making many mistakes is inevitable, but necessary to learn. Then a bond is formed between master and servant. The master no longer has to tell the servant what to do, he already knows because the will of his master in whom he serves has been learned. In the end of a master's life it has been known for him to leave his servant the greatest reward above the closest family member his entire fortune, and now the servant has become a rich man. So you see, in your effort to be rich and pursue the things of this world they are in vain, because to truly become a rich man you have to be a servant first.

The bible tells us to "Seek ye first the kingdom of Heaven and all these other things shall be added to you". Seeking the kingdom of Heaven first is indeed embracing your purpose. Your purpose is the will of the Father, and you must become a servant to Him, as Christ did when He was on Earth. When Christ embraced His servant's heart He humbled Himself to become the lowest that He may rise up and be the Highest at the right hand of God seated in Heaven. You must become a servant to your purpose, not a leader or master of it. God is the master of your destiny, not you. You must submit to His will and way, you must humble yourself before the throne of grace, and get down on your knees and wash the feet of your purpose. There is a cost to be with the Father, are you willing to pay the price? Give in to your purpose it is time to submit. As, you began the lesson of the servant's heart you will unveil the spirit of arrogance. Arrogance is the offensive display of superiority or self-importance; over-bearing pride. Now that's a mouth full. Lord Jesus, how do we overcome such a spirit? Through the Word of God, you must be delivered. You cannot master arrogance because if you are attempting to master it, in your very effort to do so show that you are arrogant. When trying to understand arrogance in a carnal way of thinking it, continues to trip you up leaving you chasing after your tail like a dog making absolutely no progress. The Word of God brings clarity, self-reflection; it allows you to see yourself through God's eyes.

Arrogance is blinding it will not allow you to see your flaws. It will continue to breed self-importance in your heart and a false sense of superiority in your mind. The only effective way is through fasting and praying will the spirit of arrogance uproot itself from your life. You have to weaken the flesh by not feeding it what it likes, and transforming the mind with the Word of God, praying without ceasing for strength to endure the transformation. In your praying you are reaching out in faith for God's help, the master. You are reaching that change in attitude that realizes you cannot do it alone.

You are on your knees; you are humbling yourself at the feet of Jesus. You are realizing your purpose is not up there in the clouds where your head has been, but at the feet of Jesus, the author and finisher of your faith. There is no Earthly remedy for arrogance. Your purpose and arrogance cannot both exist within you; one of them has got to go in order for the other to live out its purpose. There is life in the purpose God has for your life, there is only death at the end of arrogance, and it's a self-destructive life force. The Bible tells us "we can do all things through Christ who strengthen us". Not we can do all things ourselves, you cannot do it alone, but even in me telling you this, if the spirit of arrogance resides within you, it will cause you not to believe and set out to prove me wrong. We have to pull off the need to be self-important wanting to matter to a world who cannot save you.

Your purpose is bigger than you, which means that self-importance cannot be an issue for you while you pursue destiny, you will always get in your own way, therefore in the way of God. You are the servant and all that should matter is pleasing the master. Jesus was explaining to the disciples how "he that is last shall be first in the kingdom of Heaven". If, you are here on Earth chasing after everything but who you are purposed to be then in the end you would be determined as the man who sought out worldly things by avoiding his true purpose, therefore making you first in the Earth, leaving you last in the kingdom of Heaven, that's if you even make it in, but only time will tell.

Who wishes to wait to the end to know the answer to one's destination? Let's define servant, a servant is one who expresses submission, recognizance, or debt to another. We are walking the Earth like we are not in debt to God for the sacrifice of His Son to mankind. We owe Him everything, our whole lives, our total submission. He is so worthy. This kind of submission only dwells in the untapped parts of your being that lie dormant until awaken by the acknowledgement that something is indeed missing, and that is your relationship with Christ Jesus. Submitting to the cross and what it stands for comes in your discovery of Christ and the price He paid to save you. You have to get in the Word for yourself; you can't just hear about it, you must experience it for yourself. Without the illuminating power of Christ you are like a fireplace with wood (purpose) but no fire! In (1 Corinthians 12:31, 13:1-3) we learn the danger in wanting to be something you are not.

Paul was explaining to the Corinthians that wanting to simply choose who you think you ought to be in the body of Christ for the sake of fame and praise it is a destructive path, you cannot simply decide you want to be a pastor and choose your own purpose, you must be chosen by God. This is why the body of Christ is suffering we have so many operating in gifts they were never given. This is not a guessing game, you cannot fake an anointing, and either you have it or you don't.

The fruit of your labor will expose you. You must be sure. Your purpose is like a mission you are willing to accomplish without anything in return but the reward of pleasing the Father. Just knowing within yourself that what you are doing pleases Him. Remember when you were a kid and you always look for that smile on your mother or father face that reassured you that they were happy with you and your accomplishments. Just think of God and His approval of your life, that's like a million times more you feel loved, and fulfilled; Indescribable. Be careful, and wait on the Lord to reveal His purpose for your life so that you may not waste any time, or injure anyone's relationship with God because you lack what's needed. You cannot embrace a path that you are unsure about; you need to know where you are headed. Understanding how to embrace the changes that will be occurring in your life comes from studying the Word of God, no longer will you be able to process your purpose in an Earthly frame of mind, you would need to open up to what the spirit is saying to your spirit, in (Colossians 3) helps us to understand how this is possible. By taking on the character of the new man, and coming away, leaving completely the ways of fleshly living and thinking.

Not being able to comprehend your purpose will not help you if you try using it as an excuse for not completing your assignment in the Earth. You have to study and pursue what has been entrusted to you. Seek it out, knock on the doors, run after it, and want it more than life itself, because in wanting it more than life you will receive ever-lasting life. You will need to endure all types of chaos, you must learn how to persevere, and everything will not always be a box of chocolates. You must learn to abide in Christ like He is a life jacket in the middle of the ocean. In (1 John 2:28) reminds us of the importance of staying obedient to the call on our lives through Christ Jesus.

Ignoring or simply not falling in line with your purpose and living out your Christian life in your own purpose will leave you ashamed before God as He rejects you for not being obedient to His purpose for you, not your own. This I cannot stress enough, many will say what they have done in the name of Jesus, but are you in line with your God given purpose? (See Jeremiah) You cannot pick your own destiny; it has already been predestined for you. Please fall in line with the order of God. (See 1 Corinthians 12: 18) The truth is that if you are in God's Word there is no way you can miss His purpose for your life, it practically jumps off the pages. Your purpose is already inside you; just waiting awakening by the illuminating light of Christ Jesus, get in the light. Don't allow the spirit of arrogance to blind you from the truth. Arrogance causes you to feel that you know more than someone else or make you feel completely certain of your beliefs, but there is always room for corrections.

No one knows everything, I do not know everything, but what I do know I was purposed to, it is my piece of the puzzle, and my part in the body of Christ. Have you discovered yours? (Philippians 4:13) tells us "we can do all things through Christ who strengthen us". Again the purpose we must fulfill in the Earth cannot be done in your own strength, it has to be done through Christ because only through Him will it work. It cannot be by might, nor by any power you may possess, but by the Spirit says the Lord. When embracing all that God has for you, you have to take it in the spirit because there is where your battle awaits. Your battle is not with people; it is against the prince of principalities, against the powers, against the rulers of the darkness of this age, against spiritual hosts of wickedness in the Heavenly places. (See Ephesians 6:12)

To see and understand this scripture you must get in the spirit. You cannot stay outside the presence of God because you do not want to encounter the warfare. It's a part of the package, and with your purpose comes the battle, you cannot continue to run from the enemy, it's time to embrace destiny, and stand. I began to notice when I embraced my destiny I could see the good in all my storms. I could see God's purpose for my life through the things I suffered. My very personality made more sense to me than it ever did, I've always wondered why I was the way I was, and in God I discovered why. There is just something about you no one will ever understand or get, and even you may be confused about your personality, but God brings clarity, and in all you have suffered will make perfect sense in your life once your purpose is embraced. Until you can begin to allow the cracks in your life to reveal more of the light shining through them and began to dig you will forever be in the dark of confusion.

In the dark of confusion you have the mother who pushes the daughter to be who she wants her to be, the father who pressure the son to chase his purpose, given their children over to frustration and inadequacy. Living your life in disobedience leads to all types of off springs, all of which you will be held accountable. Trust God and go ahead, submit to your purpose, stop pushing it off on someone else, it's yours. Your purpose aches to be release, and many detours you take in your attempts to satisfy it with everything but submission, but when you get in God and realize the gift of the Son and the power of the Holy Spirit, you will tackle destiny like a starving lioness who hunts down her meal.

Embracing destiny comes with its own set of responsibility as well; destiny is held within you, inside the temple, your body. You have to take care of yourself, nourishing the precious gift within, being a protector of your purpose. (See 1 Corinthians 6:19) Keep your temple clean it houses the Holy Spirit who is in you. You are a carrier of precious cargo. Abiding in Christ keeps your spirit in good standing with God, yielded to the voice of the Holy Spirit within he will never mislead you. As you mature in the body of Christ the fruits of the Spirit should be evident in your life, the fruits of love, joy, peace, long suffering, kindness, goodness, faithfulness, gentleness, and self-control (See Galatians 5:22). You will need to weaken the flesh and its motives, and desires by taking away the pleasures it once craved, start by fasting.

Depending on what exactly you are struggling with before the throne of grace determines the length of your fast. Fasting will need to be with prayer and the reading of the Word of God. If you have questions or concerns about fasting speak with your pastor or spiritual advisor for a better understanding, so that it may be done correctly. Embracing the Spirit is mandatory in (Galatians 5:24,25) Paul speaks on how those who belong to Christ have put to death the sinful nature, with all its passion and desires, now you are living by the Spirit, and must line up with what the Spirit is saying.

He stresses the importance of not being or becoming conceited, provoking, and envying of others. We have to be who we are and faithfully live out our God given abilities. Being thankful and encouraging toward all those who contribute to the body of Christ. We are a family in Christ, no rivalry (Galatians 6: 1-5) should exist where the Spirit dwells. Now that you have reached the understanding of embracing destiny it is important to embrace what Paul teaches in (Ephesians 5:16-18) saying,

> Making the most of every opportunity because the days are filled with evil, therefore do not be foolish, but understand what the Lord's will is. Do not get drunk on wine, which leads to debauchery. Instead be filled with the Spirit.

Time is not on our side those days of taking your precious time will need to be left behind you. Full steam ahead into the will of the Lord, embracing your purpose is putting God will before yourself and your own needs, knowing in Him you will lack no good thing. You have to know this, and believe it with your whole heart. You will be tried. With the call of God on your life you will have to be prepared for battle.

Embrace the redemption power of God, you have been redeemed! We serve a diverse God; leave your bias in the past it cannot go where God is taking you. I spoke briefly about the many gifts in the body of Christ and cannot stress enough the importance of embracing who you are, it's sad to say that in this world we don't always appreciate each other, but in the body of Christ this is unacceptable. Hating on one another's talents and gifts is displeasing to God. We are not a kingdom set against it-self. We serve a God of order, and disorder will not be tolerated in the kingdom of Heaven. Christ says whatever we bind on Earth will be bound in Heaven, and whatever we loose on Earth will be loose in Heaven. I bind the spirit of discord in the body of Christ in the name of Jesus, it cannot stay, and it must go.

When you embrace the purpose of God for your life you embrace the fire of God. You cannot pick and choose when obeying the Lord you have to go all the way, accepting and embracing it all. In your spare time I would like you to read (1 Corinthians 12) I will quote from it briefly. I want you to understand the importance of love and how with all our special gifts and callings they are nothing if we lack love.

> In (1 Corinthians 12:27-31) Paul brings clarity to all those thinking they could get by on gifts alone. Now you are the body of Christ and each one of you is a part of it. And in the church God has appointed first of all apostles, second prophets, third teachers, then workers of miracles, also those having gifts of healing, those able to help others, those with gifts of administration, and those speaking in different kinds of tongues.
>
> Are all apostles? Are all prophets? Are all teachers? Do all work miracles? Do all have gifts of healing?

Do all speak in tongues? Do all interpret? But eagerly desire the greater gifts? You may be wondering as I did; what are the greater gifts? As I moved on to (Chapter 13) my question was answered. And now I will show you the most excellent way.

If I speak in the tongues of men and of angels, but have not love, I am only a resounding gong or a clanging cymbal. If I have the gift of prophecy and can fathom all mysteries and all knowledge, and if I have a faith that can move mountains, but have not love, I am nothing. If I give all I possess to the poor and surrender my body to the flames but have not love, I gain nothing.

Love is patient, love is kind. It does not envy, it does not boast, it is not proud. It is not rude, it is not self-seeking, it is not easily angered, it keeps no records of wrongs. Love does not delight in evil but rejoices with the truth. It always protects, always trusts, always hopes, and always perseveres. Love never fails. But where there are prophecies, they will cease; where there are tongues, they will be stilled; where there is knowledge, it will pass away. For we know in part and we prophesy in part, but when perfection comes the imperfect disappears. When I was a child, I talked like a child; I thought like a child, I reasoned like a child. When I became a man, I put childish ways behind me. Now we see but a poor reflection as in the mirror; then we shall see face to face.

Now I know in part; then I shall know fully, even as I am fully known. And now these three remain: faith, hope and love. But the greatest of these is love.

To embrace destiny is to embrace love first. Everything you do must be done in love, for God is love. Love causes us to be capable of imitating God. Paul is opening our heart to the knowledge that all these gifts will one day perish; there will be no need of them in the end, when Christ comes. You must have love. Not a memory of a gift you operated in, but love. We must not become consumed with the gifts, and not be rooted in love. Sown the seeds of the gift you operate in good soil, and be rooted in love. No exceptions.

> (We have heard the love that Paul describes as the agape love that is based on the deliberate choice of the one who loves rather than the worthiness of the one who is loved. This kind of love goes against natural human inclination. It's a giving, selfless; expect nothing in return kind of love. True love puts up with people who would be easier to give up on. Love does not give up and knows God can change lives for the better.)
>
> (Notes taken from Nelson Study Bible)

So you see, it is quite apparent that we cannot fully embrace destiny, and walk in purpose without the full embrace of love. How is it possible to help anyone without love? We work in vain if we enter back into the world without love. You cannot go forth, you are not ready. I want the full embrace of God's plan for my life not a partial. Get out everything in you not like God, allow the Holy Spirit to clean you up so you can get filled up with an over flowing amount of love. You will need it as your reentry into the world begins. The Nelson Bible gives a great breakdown of how to identify the responsibilities we must possess, as we embrace our purpose.

- To keep unity of the Spirit
- To use our abilities for the churches benefit
- To keep growing and maturing
- To put away old sinful ways

- To speak honestly and purely
- To do what the Spirit leads us to do
- To imitate God
- To walk in love
- To find out what is acceptable to the Lord
- To make the most of our time
- To be filled with the Spirit
- To submit to one another
- To have marriages that honor God
- To honor God in our families
- To demonstrates integrity in the work place
- To stand strong against the forces of evil

THE BLESSINGS WE GET TO ENJOY FOR OUR OBEDIENCE.

- Being chosen by God
- Adoption into God's family
- Acceptance before God
- Forgiveness of sins
- Insight into God's will
- An eternal inheritance
- The seal of the Spirit
- God's mercy and love
- Wisdom and Knowledge
- Divine power
- Spiritual life
- The promise of eternal kindness
- The knowledge that God's plan for us is good
- Unity and peace with all believers
- Heavenly citizenship
- Access to God through Christ

It's time to face the places where you once lived and awaken those who are yet sleeping, the friend, mother, father, brother, sister, and stranger. The Father's will is the agenda, operation soul save is now in effect, take no prisoners. All will be saved, don't take no for an answer. Get in the Spirit, stay in the Spirit, and enter the battle that has been fought and won. Good always overcomes evil. Remember with who you fight and where the battle ground is located, leave your mark in the Tween Place and place your feet on the head of the devil. Put a dent in his inventory, throw his operation into utter and total chaos.

Fight with the weapons of power you have been given, and leave no one behind. Light the fire of the Holy Spirit and blaze a trail that can be seen for miles. Get angry at what makes God angry, hate what God hates, and destroy His enemy. Enter boldly into the Tween Place, you are not that same person, you are alive, awaken, and rescued from the deep sleep of sin. You have been made new, and given power to tread over serpent, scorpions, and every dark demonic force of evil that defiles the air and the Earth.

You are a warrior in the army of God, on the front line ready to destroy, and set the Tween Place into chaos, dragging it into the Spirit with intercession and releasing blessings and new life. It's time to go to war! Code red! You are on high alert, be ever watchful, ever praying, no time to sleep or drag your feet, stay grounded and fully loaded with the Word of God. Go ahead embrace your resurrecting power given to you by Christ Jesus when He rose from the dead. You have been activated, take back your territory. Don't forget your armor; hold that sword with all your strength, and confidently know whose commander and chief. I will see you on the battle field.

www.ingramcontent.com/pod-product-compliance
Ingram Content Group UK Ltd.
Pitfield, Milton Keynes, MK11 3LW, UK
UKHW022223230420
12048UKWH00016BA/1068